My Brother Hideo Kobayashi

My Brother Hideo Kobayashi

Junko Takamizawa

Translated by James Wada

Edited with an introduction by Leith Morton

The University of Sydney East Asian Series No. 14

Wild Peony
&
Faculty of Arts and Social Science of the
University of Newcastle, NSW

Published in Sydney by Wild Peony Pty Ltd ABN 52 002 714 276
PO Box 636 Broadway NSW 2007 Australia
Fax 61 2 9566 1052

International Distribution:
University of Hawaii Press
2480 Kolowalu Street
Honolulu, Hawaii 96822, USA
Fax 1 808 988-6052

Copyright © Wild Peony Pty Ltd 2001

First Published 2001

All rights reserved. No part of this publication may be reproduced, stored in a retrieval system or transmitted in any form or by any means electronic, mechanical, photocopying, recording or otherwise without the prior permission of the publisher.

ISBN 1-876957-00-X

Printed in Australia by National Capital Printing, Canberra, A.C.T.

Acknowledgments

Permission was received from Ms Junko Takamizawa on 28 April 2001 to translate and publish her book *Ani Kobayashi Hideo*, originally published by Shinchōsha Press in Tokyo.

Photographs by courtesy of Ms Junko Takamizawa, from her private collection.

Hideo Kobayashi and his sister Junko Takamizawa as children, 1905

Hideo Kobayashi, 1980

Junko Takamizawa, 1960

Junko Takamizawa and her husband Suihō Tagawa, 1989

Contents

Acknowledgments		
Introduction		iii
Chapter 1	Nothing Could Be As Sad As This	1
Chapter 2	I Finally Had To Escape	8
Chapter 3	I Will Repay My Parents	13
Chapter 4	My Brother, The Rascal	19
Chapter 5	Eyeglasses, Eyeglasses, How Well I Can See!	25
Chapter 6	Wide Random Reading Develops A Flexibility —Apt To Be Lost In Man	31
Chapter 7	I Cannot Sermonize But Only Confess	36
Chapter 8	Why Can't We Live Together?	43
Chapter 9	To Complain Daily Is A Waste of Time	48
Chapter 10	It's Unbearable, So Don't Come	54
Chapter 11	Happiness Is So Terribly Commonplace	59
Chapter 12	People Value Feelings Most Of All	65
Chapter 13	One Can Study And Create Art Under Any Circumstances	71
Chapter 14	Don't Let Anyone Know	78
Chapter 15	I Had Failed To Repay My Mother For All Her Love	82
Chapter 16	"Norakuro" Will Remain	88
Chapter 17	Criticism Without Love Is Amiss	94
Chapter 18	A Kind Heart Is One That Feels	100

Chapter 19	One Truly Sees A Thing When Possessed By It	105
Chapter 20	A Person Who Searches His Intellect Alone Cannot Know His True Self	111
Chapter 21	I Do Things Out Of Personal Obligation Only	117
Chapter 22	Be Thankful For Something Cherished, Then Relinquish It	123
Chapter 23	I Am Prone To Injury	128
Chapter 24	How Deadly Boring It Is Talking to Men	134
Chapter 25	Because There Are Problems, So There Is Joy	139
Chapter 26	Writing Criticism Cultivates Oneself	144
Chapter 27	Each Must Believe In His Own Way	150
Chapter 28	Where Human Emotions Are Absent, So Are Truth, Beauty, And Faith	155
Chapter 29	Thank You. Please Come Again	163

Introduction

Hideo Kobayashi (1902–1983) wrote in his 1936 essay "Sakka no Kao" (The Face of the Author) that he does "not understand the tastes of those who take pleasure in discovering our ordinary, human faces on great men and heroes. It is no more than sentimentality wearing the mask of realism".[1] So it may well be that he would dislike the volume of memoirs about himself written by his younger sister Junko Takamizawa and published in 1985, two years after his death. Yet that work, translated here into English by Professor James Wada, a dedicated Kobayashi specialist of long standing, held a great deal of interest for Japanese readers when it was first published. It is not too difficult to work out why this was so. Kobayashi was the most brilliant critic of his generation and one of the best critics writing in twentieth-century Japan. In this introduction to Professor Wada's translation of Takamizawa's memoirs, I intend to provide a brief outline of Kobayashi's life and works and sketch the background to the memoirs to assist our understanding of why Hideo Kobayashi was held in such esteem by Japanese readers.

Kobayashi was born on 11 March 1902 in Kanda in downtown Tokyo.[2] His father Toyozō was born twenty-eight years earlier in 1874, and his mother Seiko was born seven years after her husband in 1881. They were married the year before Hideo was born. Toyozō originally came from Hyōgo in the west of Japan while Seiko was a native-born resident of Tokyo. Hideo was their first child. Two years later in 1904, Hideo's sister Fujiko was born. In 1928 Fujiko married Nakatarō Takamizawa (1899–1989) who is better known by his pen name of Suihō Tagawa. In 1931, under his real name, Suihō started to write a comic strip about a dog called "Norakuro" or

---

[1] Translated by Donald Keene, *Dawn to the West: Japanese Literature of the Modern Era*, Vol. 2, Poetry, Drama, Criticism (New York: Holt, Rinehart and Winston, 1983), p. 596. The original in the [Shintei] *Kobayashi Hideo Zenshū* (Collected Works; Tokyo: Shinchōsha, 1978–), Vol. 4, p. 155.
[2] Information on Kobayashi is mainly drawn from the chronology written by Hiroo Yoshida appended to the Supplementary Vol. 2 of the *Collected Works* (1979), pp. 241–74.

"Black Stray" that became a massive hit and brought him much acclaim.[3] Fujiko, using the pen name of Junko (and later Naoe), wrote not only the volume of memoirs about her brother but also dramas; however, she is best known to her contemporaries as a Christian activist. Toyozō became a professor at the Tokyo Higher Engineering School but by 1917 had established his own company, Japan Diamond, Inc.

Kobayashi was educated at a number of elite schools: the First Middle School, the First High School and Tokyo Imperial University. One of the most significant events of Kobayashi's early years was the death of his father in 1921 at the age of forty-six. Hideo was only nineteen at the time. While still at the First High School, Kobayashi began to write fiction. The stories written at this time are his only works of fiction. At university Kobayashi enrolled in the French Department, and by 1926, in his second year as a student, he was writing articles on the French poet Arthur Rimbaud. In 1920 Kobayashi had become friends with the poet Tarō Tominaga (1901–1925), and through this acquaintance in 1925 came to know the famous poet Chūya Nakahara (1907–1937). By November 1925, Kobayashi had begun a relationship with Yasuko Hasegawa, Nakahara's mistress, and late that month they rented a house to live together. This did not please Nakahara. Nor did it please Kobayashi's sister, as we can see from the memoirs, where she maintains that the relationship was a disaster for her brother.

During his years as a student at Tokyo Imperial University, Kobayashi wrote prolifically in various journals on French writers like Rimbaud and Charles Baudelaire. He also wrote an essay on the Japanese novelist Ryūnosuke Akutagawa. In 1928 at the age of twenty-six he graduated from university with a thesis on Rimbaud. By May that year he had also separated from Yasuko. In 1929 he made his debut in the literary world on being awarded second prize in a competition for works of criticism for new writers organized by *Kaizō* magazine. This essay, "Samazama naru Ishō" (Various Patterns), outlines a theory of criticism that abhors theories and ideologies, and advocates criticism based upon a living engagement with the work of art.[4] The essay was published in the magazine and immediately aroused the

---

[3] Takamizawa used characters to approximate the pronunciation of his real surname. See the reproduction of the comic strip in Isao Shimizu, *Manga no Rekishi* (Tokyo: Iwanami Shinsho, 1991), p. 137.

[4] A preliminary translation by James Wada is available in the *Tōkyō Toritsu Kagaku Gijutsu Daigaku Kiyō* (Memoirs of Tokyo Metropolitan Institute of Technology), No. 8 (January 1995), pp. 287–94. See also Paul Anderer's translation "Multiple Designs" in *Literature of the Lost Home: Kobayashi Hideo—Literary Criticisms 1924–1939* (Stanford University Press, 1995), ed. and trans. Paul Anderer, pp. 19–34. This volume contains translations of most of Kobayashi's major writings until 1939.

interest of Japanese readers, if only for its complete rejection of prevailing currents of thought.

By 1931 Kobayashi had established himself as a critic, by writing literary criticism of French and Japanese literature professionally in a variety of journals. By 1933 he was also employed as an occasional lecturer at the Bunka Gakuin academy in Tokyo. In May 1934 his essay "Various Patterns" was published in book form, and in the same month he married a woman from Matsumoto city (in Nagano Prefecture) called Kiyomi Mori (b. 1907). The newly married couple settled in Kamakura, near Tokyo. Among the major works he wrote at this time, his "Watakushi Shōsetsu Ron" (On the "I-Novel"), published between May and August 1935, is particularly well known. This examination of the major genre of contemporary Japanese fiction with frequent comparisons and references to European literature was typical of Kobayashi's broad approach to literature. The essay made the point that Japanese Naturalism was inferior to its French counterpart, and thus the "I-novel", the Japanese adaptation of the Naturalist novel, was fatally flawed.

For the next ten years or so Kobayashi concentrated on European rather than Japanese literature, with Dostoevsky his chief interest, although he still contributed occasional pieces on Japanese literature to various periodicals. Kobayashi also penned various pieces on theoretical or general issues relating to literature, such as "Shisō to Jisseikatsu" (Thought and Real Life) published in April 1936 and "Bunka to Buntai" (Culture and Style) published in May 1937. In March 1937 his only child, a daughter, Haruko, was born.

In 1938 Kobayashi visited China as special correspondent for the *Bungei Shunjū* journal, and wrote several pieces on the military situation unfolding on the Asian continent. However, as he noted in his May 1938 article "Kōshū" (Hangzhou), "I decided not to go to the front line... the desire to know the underside to war, a kind of curiosity to lay bare the war—as soon as this struck me, it disappeared... I cannot face the extreme situation of war with a balanced mind."[5] Kobayashi, in general, supported the actions of his government but, as Edward Seidensticker observes, commenting on Kobayashi's reaction to Pearl Harbor, "There is nothing of the jingoist in [him]." He further notes that during the war years Kobayashi "spoke in subdued tones".[6]

Also, in 1938 Kobayashi was appointed to the position of professor at Meiji University where he had been lecturing for some time. Kobayashi's translations of French literature had been appearing for many years, principally his translations of André Gide, Arthur Rimbaud, Paul Valéry and

---

[5] *Collected Works*, Vol. 4, p. 308.
[6] Edward Seidensticker, *This Country, Japan* (Tokyo, New York: Kodansha International, 1979), p. 180.

Charles Baudelaire. In August that year Kobayashi's translation of Rimbaud's *Une Saison en enfer* was published in paperback.

In May 1939, his major volume *Dosutoefusukii no Seikatsu* (The Life of Dostoevsky) was published. As Donald Keene has remarked, the importance of Kobayashi's work on Dostoevsky does not lie in its originality —Kobayashi freely admitted that he had utilized several secondary sources written in Western languages. Rather, it lies in the fact that "a Japanese intellectual should have written with skill and assurance about a European author—neither disqualifying himself because of his nationality nor attempting to impart any specifically Japanese quality to his account."[7] Hiroo Yoshida notes that from late 1941 Kobayashi had begun to display a distinct fondness for classical art—not only painting but also sculpture and pottery. Keeping in mind his father's background in engineering and diamond production, and also the difficult climate of the times, this may not seem so unusual.[8] However, Kobayashi kept his interest in art, and developed into a major critic, collector and all-round connoisseur.

In the prewar period Kobayashi was involved in a number of literary debates about the relationship between life and art, primarily with the critic and novelist Hakuchō Masamune (1879–1962) and the novelist Shigeharu Nakano (1902–1979). Kobayashi's position was complex but he did not accept any simplistic equation of life with the art and ideas borne from life. This led him to oppose what we now describe as "identity politics", the notion that the circumstances of an artist's life or his or her beliefs determine the quality or nature of their art. Consequently, he strongly opposed any criticism or evaluation that derived from an ideology. He also wrote extensively on two authors: Naoya Shiga (1883–1971) and Kan (or Hiroshi) Kikuchi (1888–1948). The reason why Kobayashi championed these two writers was his dislike of fiction that was overtly intellectual or psychological: a distrust of conceptuality as a literary device. His enthusiasm for Kikuchi especially provoked opposition, as Kikuchi was read then and now in Japan as a mere storyteller, a popular novelist of no real literary significance.[9]

During 1942 and 1943 Kobayashi changed direction by publishing a large number of essays on classical Japanese literature, a subject that he had avoided until then. His style changed also. His early writings were renowned for their difficulty, Kobayashi's delight in paradoxical expressions being famous. However, his articles on such classical masterpieces as the *Heike*

---

[7] Keene, *Dawn to the West*, Vol. 2, p. 593.
[8] *Collected Works*, Supplementary Vol. 2, p. 255.
[9] See Edward Seidensticker's discussion of these issues in *This Country, Japan*, pp. 160–7, and translations of these essays in Anderer, *Literature of the Lost Home*.

Monogatari (Tale of the Heike), published in July 1942, and on *Tsurezuregusa* (Essays in Idleness), published the next month, were written in a much simpler, even poetic style. Throughout these years, Kobayashi travelled to China three times, for Greater East Asian Writers' conferences, not always by choice or his own initiative. He was also elected secretary of the critics' section of the Japan Patriotic Writers' Association in 1942. In the last two years of the war, Kobayashi mainly worked on his study of Mozart, which he had planned from 1942.

In May 1946 his mother died at the age of sixty-six. The next month Kobayashi was named in a literary journal as one of the writers bearing some degree of responsibility for the war, that is, as someone who had actively collaborated in the war effort. In August he resigned from his professorship at Meiji University, ostensibly over an internal matter. Around the same time, he fell from the platform of Suidōbashi station in Tokyo, sustaining minor injuries, and went to Yugawara to recuperate. In her memoirs, his sister claimed that he was drunk at the time. In 1947 his volume on Mozart was published to considerable acclaim. In the same year, Kobayashi published the first of a series of articles on Japanese painters, reflecting his interest in art, which, to some degree, came to overshadow his concern with literature.

In 1948, Kobayashi conducted a published dialogue with the Nobel Prize physicist Hideki Yukawa (1907–1981) in which he stated that Dostoevsky was his own alter ego; Yukawa took Einstein as his.[10] In October the following year, Kobayashi made public his view of life by publishing a book of the same name, *Watakushi no Jinseikan* (My View of Life), a re-writing of a lecture delivered the previous year.[11]

By 1950 Kobayashi had won such acclaim that an eight-volume collected works commenced publication in September, and in March the following year this set was awarded the Geijutsuin Prize. Since 1948, Kobayashi had been publishing in instalments *Gohho no Tegami* (The Letters of Van Gogh); in June 1952 the serialized articles were collected and published as *Gohho no Tegami—Shokan ni yoru Denki* (The Letters of Van Gogh—A Biography in Letters). In January the following year, this volume was awarded the Yomiuri Literary Prize for criticism. From December 1952 to July 1953, Kobayashi travelled throughout Europe and the US. In the following year, he began to serialize his *Kindai Kaiga* (Modern Painting) in the

---

[10] For details, see James Wada, "Jiro Aoyama's and Hideo Kobayashi's Understanding of 'Intuitive Seeing'", *Memoirs of Tokyo Metropolitan Institute of Technology*, No. 7 (December 1993), pp. 162–3.
[11] James Wada has translated this into English. See "My View of Life", *Memoirs of Tokyo Metropolitan Institute of Technology*, No. 12 (September 1998), pp. 213–45.

Shinchō journal. The complete volume was finally published in 1958 and awarded the Noma Literary Prize the same year.

Donald Keene, who resided in Japan for much of this period, has commented on the near idolatrous way in which Kobayashi was seen by the Japanese public: "He had become, even during his lifetime, an almost mythical figure, the touchstone against whom other critics were judged and the pride of the world of Japanese letters."[12] Keene points out that Kobayashi's tastes were adopted by many critics, so influential was he.[13]

This influence was confirmed by Kobayashi's final masterpiece, his study of the eighteenth-century thinker Norinaga Motoori (1730–1801), published in 1977 when he was seventy-five, after some twelve years of writing. It was awarded the Grand Prix for Japanese Literature the following year. Prior to the serialization of this work, which commenced in 1965, Kobayashi had written on various subjects, notably the French philosopher Henri Bergson, and he also undertook a brief trip to the Soviet Union in 1963. He was in great demand as a lecturer and frequently spoke on radio. In 1964 a collection of essays he wrote for the general public over the previous five years was published under the title of *Kangaeru Hinto* (Hints for Thinking) and became a best seller. By this time, his earlier major books had been reprinted several times, with most of them being available in paperback. In November 1967 he was decorated by the government with the award of the Medal of Culture.

The book on Motoori is generally seen as the culmination of his career as a critic. A long, difficult study of a most profound and complex thinker, the book is perhaps more praised than read. Since Kobayashi's death in March 1983, his style of literary and intellectual criticism has fallen out of favour but there is no doubt that he will be regarded by history as one of the intellectual giants of twentieth-century Japan.

Junko Takamizawa's volume of memoirs *My Brother Kobayashi Hideo* (Ani Kobayashi Hideo) was published in 1985. The book harbours no literary pretensions; it is simply a set of memoirs about her distinguished brother. As we can see in Professor Wada's translation, Junko Takamizawa is concerned overwhelmingly with personal matters: the impact of her brother on her family and her own life. So she treats in some detail his relationship with Yasuko Hasegawa, or Sakiko, as she was known, and spends much time discussing the trials and tribulations her mother was subjected to by her only son. It is a commonplace that the intellectual stature of great men often

---

[12] Keene, *Dawn to the West*, Vol. 2, p. 610.
[13] *Ibid.*

is not matched by their moral character but, although Takamizawa documents her brother's unreflecting reliance on his family for domestic tranquillity and comfort, he does not emerge from her narrative as someone whose character in private life was all that different from his public persona. Indeed, Takamizawa's love and affection for her brother appear undisguised in her account.

If Japanese readers expected an exposé that would show a severe schism between the public and the private selves, then they were obviously disappointed with the book. But if, as is more likely, they expected that Kobayashi would emerge like most Japanese intellectuals as a man with strong ties to his family, especially his mother, then they would not have been at all surprised. Nevertheless, the value of Takamizawa's memoirs lies in this most intimate and personal portrait of a great critic and thinker. Despite Kobayashi's own strictures against the sentimentality that seeks to discover a hidden face behind the public person, we can easily sympathize with the desire of readers to know more about the man behind the severe intellectual mask we find in his works. If the revelation that in his private life he was no different to most people is the one that strikes readers most forcefully, then we can be grateful for this; for this fact alone raises several interesting questions about the sources of inspiration that lead to genius. In fact, this very revelation only confirms Kobayashi's own suspicion of a viewpoint that seeks to create psychological explanations to cover every contingency of human nature.

Early in his career, Kobayashi wrote a severe critique of the novelist Ton Satomi's (1888–1983) fictionalized portrait of his family, a thinly disguised attempt by Satomi to conceal the reality beneath the veneer of fiction. What seemed to annoy Kobayashi most was the superior, psychologizing tone adopted by Satomi, pretending that he could somehow stand apart from his subject—his own family. Kobayashi's literary criticism is, as Paul Anderer has rightly pointed out, suffused with a "personal, ironic tone" that "uncovered the critic as the heretofore hidden but proper subject of criticism".[14] The critic then is his ideas, a notion analogous to the Buddhist belief that a man is simply the sum total of his actions. The portrait that is painted of Kobayashi by his sister rarely deals with Kobayashi's ideas. Takamizawa quotes other authorities on Kobayashi's historical significance as a critic. What most interests her is her brother in his social role as a family member and, to a degree, as an emotional being. In other words, not ideas but emotions tend to make up the constituent elements of her portrait. This is not psychologizing in the sense that Kobayashi himself warned against; it is something simpler, more easily understood. If this aspect of Kobayashi's character strikes us as commonplace, then, we can recognize here the

---

[14] Anderer, *Literature of the Lost Home*, p. 7.

quotidian self of humanity, the common features of the face we see when we look into a mirror. And, perhaps, there is something comforting in this.

At least, that is my own reaction to this intimate portrait of a great thinker by his sister. For such a view puts paid to a rarely expressed but commonly held belief that Japanese, especially Japanese intellectuals, really are different from non-Japanese, that their private selves conceal a quite different reality from that seen in their cosmopolitan writings. It is as if the public face and the private are two masks, and the mask covering the private face conceals far more than that covering the public face. Such logic is nonsense but a nonsense that is sometimes taken more seriously than it should be. We now have translations and studies of Kobayashi in English that reveal a good deal of the public face to us—a complex, ironic, paradoxical, intellectual face that often seems remote yet somehow familiar, a face remarkably similar to some of our own feisty, paradoxical critics. The private face revealed here, with no attempt at concealment, in plain, conversational Japanese, reveals a less remote and even more familiar face, despite the obvious differences between the West and Japan. The social and familial expectations imposed upon only sons in Japan resurface again and again, and the instances of pride and disappointment of mother and sister in their son and brother are equally transparent in Takamizawa's narrative. But, underneath this, the sense of familiarity to our own sons and brothers is manifested equally powerfully.

To a degree, this is due to Kobayashi's sister perceiving her brother as such. But, clearly, the family ties and obligations, and her clear consciousness of them, dictate that this must be so. The familiarity arises as much out of his sister's expectations and perceptions as in her brother's behaviour. In this respect, the book is also a portrait of the sister, and, to a lesser degree, the mother, which also adds to our interest. Junko Takamizawa appears as a character in her own text—the name "Junko" after all was a name later given to her in the belief that it would bring her good fortune. This smaller portrait of the sister with some intellectual ambitions struggling to make an impact in the face of the all-encompassing achievements of her older brother holds no little fascination for the reader.

In short, this supremely unambitious set of memoirs adds considerably to our knowledge of Hideo Kobayashi in his quotidian roles as a brother and son. And we must be grateful to Professor Wada for making it available to us in English. If the portrait may seem at times a little too partisan (surely Yasuko Hasegawa is not solely to blame for the difficulties of that relationship), then this is understandable in a narrative that does not intend anything other than a subjective, intimate, and ultimately affectionate memoir of a much loved brother.

Leith Morton
Newcastle, Australia

Chapter 1
Nothing Could Be As Sad As This

On 20 March 1921 our father, Toyozō, left this earth at the age of forty-seven. My elder brother, Hideo, was about to turn nineteen.

Since he was in the midst of his entrance exams for the elite First Higher School (now the Liberal Arts Department of the University of Tokyo), Hideo was in a tense state at the time; but our father's death marked the beginning of his adult life. Or perhaps better put, it was the turning point of his life. That is, it brought change to all in the family, the responsibility of which he had to bear.

I was almost seventeen at the time, but I was still pampered and uninformed of our family finances. Though I grieved our father's death, I was not aware of how deeply it would affect our livelihood.

Father had just returned from Osaka when he came down with a high fever. Learning it was typhoid, we had him hospitalized, but just when we began to be relieved because he showed signs of improving, pneumonia set in.

A call awakened us in the middle of the night. Our mother, Hideo and I rushed by rickshaw through the dark streets to the hospital. I remember trembling in shock and dread as we swayed in the rickshaw.

Father was in a coma, with an oxygen mask over his mouth. Each time Hideo or I called out "Father, father", he managed to respond by opening his eyes wide, but how aware he was of our presence, we couldn't tell.

I don't remember how many hours passed. Then a nurse entered hurriedly and exited. The doctor came and pressed our father's chest repeatedly. Then he stopped breathing. It looked to me that his breathing had ceased because the doctor pressed on his chest.

Morning.

We two—Hideo and I—stood blankly near the window of the empty waiting-room. Outside, in the meantime, the wind had turned violent, the sky had become yellow from the dust, and the tree branches swayed savagely almost breaking in two.

Hideo suddenly broke the long silence by saying, "Nothing could be as sad as this", and blinked his eyes. I nodded and, as if prompted by his words, I remember tears welling in my eyes.

Hideo had always far excelled me in intelligence, ability, breadth of knowledge, and thinking. Although we possibly resembled each other in perseverance and quietness, in all other respects we were opposites. An exception was that we ate fish equally awkwardly. We left on the dish the fish we had clumsily poked at with our chopsticks as a shameful aftermath. Our mother used to scold us, but this apathetic habit remained. Or, perhaps eating fish properly is not an acquired habit, since some from early childhood can pick the bones clean. My problem was, perhaps, that I didn't like fish; but Hideo—who insisted on eating only fresh fish—ate as clumsily as I.

Another exception was that we both refused to eat raw oysters, regardless of how fresh and delicious they were. After our father's death, father explained that he had contracted typhoid from eating raw oysters while aboard an oyster boat in Osaka. This frightened both of us so much that we could never eat raw oysters.

Immediately after father died on 20 March, the First Higher School announced the entrance exam results, which showed that Hideo had qualified. But father had passed away before he could see this glorious moment, which probably disappointed Hideo to no small degree.

For a girl nearly seventeen, I was naive and uninformed about our father's work. I only knew that he had founded the Nihon Diamond Corporation, owned a shop in the Ginza, and had started a small factory in Shiba-Shirokane which made jewellery with precision machines. Hideo, on the other hand, knew father's work quite well. He had actually helped father in his work. He also knew of the deep financial debts our family had incurred, so father's death was no doubt a devastating blow to him.

It was only much later that I discovered father had graduated from the machinery section of the Tokyo Higher School of Technology (now Tokyo Institute of Technology). He became associate professor there and was then sent by the Ministry of Education to Europe and America to study the precious metals industries. After his return, he was appointed head of Mikimoto Precious Metals Factory. Soon after, President Kōkichi Mikimoto selected him to tour European and American jewellery factories. On this trip, at a diamond-cutting factory in Antwerp, Belgium, he learned his basic skills.

In 1913 father travelled to Belgium and became the first in Japan to import machines and techniques for diamond cutting and polishing, to perfect methods for inlaying precious stones in jewellery, a technique unknown in Japan, and tooling claws to fix stones in rings. Father contributed in this area to Japan's industry in no small way, pioneering the techniques for the production of Western jewellery.

He left Mikimoto Precious Metals to start his own company. To do this, he invested all the family resources, only the house we lived in remained to us after his death.

"A writer is a kind of artisan who creates writing," Hideo used to tell me and others. Hideo admired artisans who fully absorbed themselves in their work regardless of the suffering and cost. In this sense, Hideo respected our father who had a deep feeling for research and a taste for artisanship.

Above all, father enjoyed making things, and evidently owned many patents. Only later did I learn that he was the first in Japan to make ruby gramophone needles. Hideo too—having inherited his father's blood—during his primary school days, often liked to help father make things at the nearby factory.

Our mother died in 1946 at the age of sixty-six, but I was unable to be at her deathbed on 27 May. We, the Takamizawa family, had returned from our place of refuge in Nagano prefecture to war-devastated Tokyo at the war's end the previous year. However, unable to return to our Ogikubo house, which had been rented to a cousin during the period of our evacuation, we moved into the second floor of our cousin's office. There, our aunt in Tokyo phoned to say that my mother had passed away. I was shocked.

From some time before, I had not gone to Kamakura to see her; and, though she had been sick, I had not been informed that she had become bedridden or that she was critically ill. Thus, her death came as a total surprise to me. I wanted to go immediately to Kamakura, but since I knew I would have to stay overnight and take my son who was almost four with me, it took time to prepare before I could hasten to Kamakura.

When I opened the door to the Kamakura house, Hideo was the first to come to meet me. "Oh, you finally arrived." He looked at me as if he was wearied from waiting for my arrival, but all the same he seemed relieved to see me. All during my train trip to Kamakura, I had felt so sorry about our mother, but seeing how far more grieved Hideo was, tears came to my eyes.

She was dead, her neck slightly turned to one side, her face tilted downward. I looked intently into her small face, and tearfully apologized to her.

Both Hideo and I had been irresponsible—living our lives as we pleased—often bringing loneliness and grief to our mother, who had been widowed and suffered in poor health. During her twenty-five years of widowhood, she had rarely tasted actual joy, satisfaction, or happiness—though now I wonder if this wasn't due more to her own gloomy character.

At the crematorium, I saw Hideo press endearingly to his breast the urn containing her bones wrapped in white cloth. I could sense his sorrow only too well, and I found myself unable to control my tears.

The circumstances at the time of Hideo's death contrasted with those of my parents. At Hideo's deathbed, I felt there was nothing sudden or fearful and no need to apologize. Nor did I burst into tears. I merely felt a sudden loss of strength as if part of me was missing.

Such was the case, perhaps, because for two weeks I had known of Hideo's hopeless situation and had already been grieving. He passed away suddenly just when I had begun to understand him as a brother. He had once seemed so distant but had drawn so much closer to me as we aged that I could truly call him brother.

It was early 1983. Though from early February I had visited him in the hospital, and found him usually asleep, he had managed to open his eyes on occasions to look my way, but said nothing. To avoid disturbing or fatiguing him, I did not talk to him. I sat heavy-hearted next to my sister-in-law, Kiyomi, quietly watching Hideo's face.

"What is he thinking? If only he would speak, I would know," she said many times to break the silence, and I would nod and sigh.

Without saying another word, Hideo died quietly, in a way that typified his long-suffering ways. He had always been quiet by nature, and never offered excuses. Exhausted, Hideo had perhaps casually thought, "I couldn't care less now. It matters little whether I speak or not, or whether people understand or not."

Hideo once said to me, "Everyone has secrets he wants kept hidden." It seems he had held onto his secrets to the end, then quietly died with them. In the same way he had silently endured the pains of intravenous feeding and dialysis with patience; he bore his thoughts without expressing them. Though he may have desired to, he probably could not find the right words.

He probably had much more to say and write. Like an iceberg, he always revealed only a small portion, and kept the vast remainder deeply submerged. He probably had no regrets that he had only managed to express a part of himself in life, and never fretted or complained about his desire to reveal more of himself. Though exhausted and unable to say any more, it seemed to me that he remained to the end at peace. I tried to absorb this understanding into myself to compose myself but it did not help.

Kiyomi told me that when she was alone and sitting quietly by his bedside, Hideo had looked into her eyes with tears pouring down his cheeks.

"What thoughts had brought these tears? What was it he wanted to say?" she asked me in tears herself. Of course, Hideo's tears had expressed an inexpressible emotion: deep love for her, gratefulness for her care, and sorrow for having to part from her.

Nonetheless, Hideo's final, month-long silence was baffling. Perhaps that silence contained a secret that comes to one before death, which no living soul could possibly comprehend.

I can no longer listen to Hideo's words, of course. But I can re-read his writings and appreciate them, pick up what I had missed, understand what previously I could not. Thus, I believe, I can hear his words and see his person anew.

About ten years ago, not having a poetry card written in brush by Hideo, I urged him to write one for me.

He wrote in brushstroke "Cool head, warm feet. Hideo."

Many years before, the Christian poet Mitsumasa Shimazaki had similarly requested that Hideo write a poetry card to commemorate a donation for the handicapped. This poet laughingly explained to me that Hideo had written, "Cool head, warm feet." For some reason this sounded comical to us both.

Reminded of it, I asked Hideo rather foolishly, "Why do you always write with your brush 'Cool head, warm feet'?"

Hideo answered, "It's so common, yet most important." Many had considered Hideo a man of commonsense, who valued the matters in life that seem commonplace and obvious. In this sense, Hideo disdained the *intelli* of Japan. *Intelli*, now a Japanese word, means a know-it-all, Hideo explained.

Perhaps I, too, belong to this category of *intelli*, I take lightly matters considered commonsense or ordinary and look down on them as vulgar. I regard words such as "Cool head, warm feet" as comical and laugh aloud.

Only recently have his words penetrated deep inside me.

In his memory, I keep this poetry card in my room, mounted in a round frame, along with a large photograph of Hideo that my sister-in-law gave me the day after the family funeral. It shows his healthy face, wide-open eyes, and lips pressed in firm satisfaction. In the background there is a clown's face being painted by George Rouault on his favourite palette, and beside it is a large, white Yi Dynasty pot that Hideo loved. The portrait was taken in 1980, three years before his death. In front of it are twenty-odd telegrams of condolence which had arrived during my four days' absence following Hideo's death, and some flowers I replace every three or four days. The flowers I pick from my garden—roses, columbine, verbenas, gerberas, stokesia, etc.—are perhaps not his favourites, but I know he would accept them.

In addition to these telegrams of condolence, I received some thirty letters expressing grief and ten monetary gifts. Some of them, of course, were from dear friends, but the majority were from people I had only met once in the countryside, or people I hadn't heard from for over ten years. Some were even strangers.

A neighbourhood woman brought over three large cattleya flowers and requested that they be placed before Hideo's photograph. A friend, an editor of a Christian magazine, sent a pot of beautiful white clematis flowers, and signed it together with a friend of mine in Scotland.

Even two months after Hideo's death, some people were still sending money for flowers, or brought bouquets, or delivered elegiac poems composed for Hideo. One student, deeply hurt and saddened by Hideo's death, wrote that he always carried with him the magazine titled "Hideo Kobayashi: Special Memorial Edition" published by *Shinchōsha*, re-reading it over and over.

Then in early June, three months after Hideo's death, when I travelled to Kamaishi city, Iwate prefecture, I met a young man who had graduated the previous year from Kokugakuin University in Tokyo. Now a Japanese-language teacher in a high school in Iwaizumi, Iwate prefecture, he happened to be in his hometown in Kamaishi city for the weekend.

He told me that he had read Hideo's works at university, and had been so deeply impressed that he had re-read them over and over again. Holding back his tears, he said,

> I never met Hideo Kobayashi or talked to him. Still, when I heard of his death, I was stunned. All seemed to end for me. I felt as if I had lost my dearest companion, and, to my surprise, I still find myself grief-stricken. I wasn't aware how deeply Hideo Kobayashi's writings—his words—had penetrated into my soul.

How foolish is man.

"When one is finally willing to care, one's parents have passed away" is an ironical *senryū* verse, which rings painfully not only to Hideo and me, but to many others.

The household of an acquaintance, who is the mother of three daughters in their late teens, appeared quite harmonious; but, in fact, she was constantly quarrelling, and at odds with them. My friend poured out her anguish to me, no longer able as a mother to endure the girls' selfishness and wilful behaviour. The daughters too, often clashed amongst themselves out of selfishness and came to me, complaining that their mother lacked understanding and showed partiality. This disturbed me, and I used to think then that if only they could compromise and forgive.

Later, the mother was hospitalized with cancer, and eventually died. The three daughters reacted most extraordinarily. They gathered around her body and cried their hearts out. None of them looked up and noticed me in the room. Seeing them, I felt anger instead of sympathy stir inside me.

I started to admonish them. If they were so grieved, why hadn't they treated her with more kindness and joy when she was alive, instead of hating her and bickering with her?

Then I realized that they were grieving, perhaps not necessarily at their mother's death, but because they regretted having treated her so ill. Though I thought their penitence noble, how tragic and foolhardy they were, unable to mourn in sincerity.

Hideo and I had treated our mother similarly in a foolhardy, tragic way, though not to the extent of bickering with her and despising her. In addition, I felt I had treated Hideo in a similar way.

Dazed for over two months following Hideo's funeral, disappointed, grieving, despondent at losing someone so dear to me, I felt a growing need to apologize to Hideo.

Such are human beings. When it is too late, we understand our true feelings towards each other, and awaken to our wrongdoings. How pathetic we humans are.

Chapter 2
I Finally Had To Escape

In my childhood, I thought Hideo a spiteful brat. Though he often helped me in primary school days with arithmetic and Japanese—as we studied with our small desks side by side in the same room—he would shout angrily whenever I was slow or failed to understand him. As he became engrossed in something, he would be completely indifferent to me, which made it difficult for me to draw near and endear myself to him. He was always a brother to be feared.

Admittedly, however, I admired the voracity with which Hideo read, not only at his desk but wherever I happened to see him; and it was his example that I probably copied. From my primary school days, I also read so much that my parents and teachers often had to caution me. Besides well-known fairy tales or children's books, I engrossed myself in "red books", or tearjerker stories, like those in comic books for girls today. Despite this type of reading, I give credit to Hideo for the joy I have in reading to this day.

From Hideo's younger days, however, I constantly resented Hideo who behaved so irresponsibly as the eldest son to our widowed mother—though in my immaturity and complete naïveté, I too must admit my own irresponsibility to her during those days.

In 1924, the three of us moved into a small, four-room rental in Kōenji after our mother had finally recuperated from two and half years of illness. Hideo took the eight-mat room for his study and I the three-mat room adjoining the entrance of my room—but he seldom spent his time at home. If he occasionally came home, he returned late at night, bringing four or five of his coterie-magazine buddies with him, with whom he drank sake and had loud discussions. When the sake ran low, he would order me to go to buy more. Nearly in tears I would walk into the dark street. He was never up in the morning as I hastily left for college, and when I returned, he was almost always out again.

How lonely my widowed mother was, not finding the slightest occasion to talk to Hideo at leisure. Since she was weak in health and unable to work much, she had only Hideo to rely on. I grew angry and then began to detest

Hideo for behaving so selfishly, oblivious to our mother's needs. I wrote a detailed letter to Professor Yutaka Tatsuno, his French literature professor and mentor at Tokyo Imperial University, describing Hideo's selfishness, asking that he reason with him and tell him about the pitiful state of our mother. But I never got a reply, nor did I find out if he had talked to Hideo or not.

In particular, I felt Hideo ruthless when he totally abandoned my mother and me to live with Yasuko Hasegawa, the poet Chūya Nakahara's lover. Fuming bitterly inside, I helped Hideo pack. As I watched a now thin mother patiently sorting and stacking his clothing and undershirts, I bore a grudge against my brother.

Hideo had been forced to sell most of our valuables—my father's antiques, old hanging-scrolls, and books—for anything he could get in order to maintain our livelihood. Now, for his new household, he sold the last remaining items, a beautiful glass-doored bookcase with drawers (the upper section being bookshelves and the lower section drawers) that almost reached the ceiling, and all the books inside. These included an entire set of the Japanese classics that belonged to my father.

After Hideo moved out, the house seemed to be an empty dwelling, as if every item had been disposed of.

For the first six months, Hideo's new household was within walking distance, so I often dropped by, and he frequently visited us. However, each time Yasuko's illness grew worse, he moved elsewhere. He moved to Kamakura, then Zushi, and Meguro ward—during which time I rarely saw him. A year after that he finally moved to a small rented house in Yato, Higashi Nakano, and I saw him again. The house was owned by the scholar of English literature Tai Matsumoto, who wrote mystery novels, and his wife, Keiko, an acquaintance of mine, who had helped me on many previous occasions. So, it was to the same housing complex in Yato where I had visited the Matsumotos many times that Hideo and Yasuko came to live.

In the same complex, Nakatarō Takamizawa (pen-name Suihō Tagawa), a painter of abstract art, lived. I met him there and later married him.

Yasuko's illness had grown considerably worse by then. And since Hideo had already instructed me that she had fits after seeing me, I used to return home after seeing the Matsumotos without visiting Hideo.

It was in May, less than three months after moving there, that Hideo disappeared, totally abandoning Yasuko in the Yato house. My mother and I were very worried, until I received a letter from Hideo, written from an Osaka temple. Reading the letter, I could see that Hideo had drawn much closer to me. His letter was indescribably pathetic. He opened himself to me as never before, pouring himself out. His letter expressed a deep, brotherly love from the depths of his misery and emotional fatigue.

The thin, meagre brown envelope had "confidential" penned on it, but not his name. I recognized by the writing that it was from Hideo. The letter itself was scrawled in ink on two manuscript sheets.

c/o Myōkō Temple
3, 8-chōme, Tennōjidani-machi
Osaka

Dear Fujiko,

I finally had to escape, not because of a whim or anything like that—I couldn't help myself. I think you know how much I have suffered, at least to the degree that you can get a faint veiled glimpse. I, in fact, tried to the utmost of my power. What foolish suffering it was! I hope that all will end now.

This is a temple. It's a splendid Nichiren temple. I am like a prisoner escaped from prison. Squatting on the wide veranda my mind is blank. A snake is swimming lithely in the pond.

If I have done wrong, god will punish me; if I am innocent, god will be good to me. Anyway, I'm terribly tired. I'm looking into the sunlight and I wonder: is the spring sunlight this colour?

Don't worry about me. Tell mother not to worry. If Sakiko [Yasuko] should drop by, don't give her a hearing. Don't say anything to others about my leaving her, because this will only lead to trouble. Ignore them, though they may not necessarily blame me.

At the moment I have no plans. If the temple will have me, I will remain here. For a while I won't return to Tokyo. If I can find a job, I will work.

Anyway, don't worry. If it is only your brother you can trust then believe only in me. I have certainly worried you. I am tired, but I'll write again.

Leave the house in Yato as it is. I still have to pay this month's rent. I will, when I make some money.

Hideo

P.S. At the end of the month, go to the Yato house, without letting Sakiko see you. She probably won't be there, anyway. No, I'll write to you about this again. Now, I am tired mentally; I can hardly hold the pen.

Farewell for now.

Where in Osaka does Uncle Nishimura live?

Fujiko was my original given name, and Sakiko was Yasuko Hasegawa's before my mother re-named us Junko and Yasuko after consulting a name-omen reader. Uncle Nishimura is my father's younger brother, whose son is cousin Kōji Nishimura.

At long last, I understood through this letter how much Hideo had suffered, and what his innermost feelings had been.

After this, he wandered about for nearly a year in the Kansai area, going from Osaka to live in Nara, and from there to Kobe and Kyoto, cared for by the writer Naoya Shiga in Nara, Uncle Shimizu in Kyoto, and other friends. It was an unsettled life, but nonetheless he managed to read extensively, write for magazines, and give lectures. He wrote to me several times. Each letter revealed to me deeper insights into Hideo.

"Brothers and sisters reared together become strangers", it is said. Brothers and sisters reared and living together under the same roof grow intimate, but upon reaching adulthood and having to make a livelihood, they meet less frequently, lose ties, and become estranged. In my case, however, since I can remember, Hideo and I grew up together as the only two children, but he always seemed distant from me. It was only after his tragic romance, his escape to Kansai and his letters to me that he began to appear as a brother. Though unquestionably unsettled and a vagabond, he had in the end begun to confide in me as a trustworthy brother should.

About that time, Nakatarō Takamizawa proposed to me, which put me in a quandary. I had plans and dreams and felt rather insecure marrying an unknown man who was struggling financially and who faced an uncertain future. Moreover, I had to think of my mother who was in poor health. I could not decide alone. I wrote to Hideo for advice.

He wrote a lengthy letter describing his standing regarding Sakiko, and concluded it with:

> You are fortunate to have Takamizawa loving you so. Remember how rare it is for anyone to possess such love, a thing which one is apt to forget. Takamizawa is a good-natured man, not in the popular sense of being weak-willed, but in that he is pure-hearted.

This lengthy letter endeared Hideo to me, I became ever so much closer to him. I was grateful that amid the misery of his own tragic love, he had taken me so deeply to heart, troubling himself to write about my marriage. Based on this letter, I decided to marry.

Hideo had looked beyond the usual marriage conditions a family considers, such as the groom's finances, future career prospects and university credentials, and had considered only Takamizawa's purity of heart.

Hideo had judged correctly. Thanks to Hideo, I have enjoyed a successful marriage and been able to accomplish my goals in life. I can now say without exaggeration, "All my fortunes until now and my happiness at present I owe to Hideo." Yet, I ask myself why hadn't I ever thanked Hideo?

After Hideo's death, I came to realize how his few words of advice had given me a new lease on life and the injustice that I had done Hideo by not once thanking him.

"Thank you. I owe everything to you," I ought to have said, bowing deeply. Not only for his advice. I had learned much from his writings and the innumerable conversations we shared as he sat opposite me sipping sake at suppertime in his Kamakura home—occasions I so looked forward to. So many of his words had touched my inner soul.

In my lectures and short writings, I have often quoted what he taught me, putting his words to good use. When I do, fans of Hideo Kobayashi express their appreciation; some envy me for having such a brother.

At this moment, my memories of Hideo seem beautiful. From these, I hope to understand the true image of Hideo, my brother.

Chapter 3
I Will Repay My Parents

In the spring of 1982, a year before my brother died, when Hideo was undergoing a complete physical examination, I received a call at my home from Haruko, Hideo's only daughter, in Kamakura.

The doctor had asked her if her father had ever contracted whooping cough, measles, or mumps in his childhood. She called me saying: "Only you, Auntie, know about his childhood." So in the end, as she stated, I was the last one alive who would know. I felt a certain loneliness draw in upon me. About his childhood, however, particularly his medical history, I remembered little. Even about myself, I could only surmise if I had ever contracted measles or whooping cough. Mumps I remembered, because I had it when I was old enough to remember.

I could merely reply that since vaccines for measles and whooping cough were unavailable then, he had probably had these. As for mumps, I was uncertain.

A more sensitive person with a keener memory would remember what his parents had said; but I, who was somewhat insensitive, could not recollect at all, even had my mother told me. If Hideo himself didn't remember, how could I be expected to?

I did remember my mother saying that as a baby Hideo was pale and delicate, with a girlish face, so that until he was two or three people often mistook him for a girl. Furthermore, since he was a sissy, he often cried. A photograph taken in July 1904, when he was two years and three months, shows him wearing a white bonnet like the one worn by the deity of wealth Daikoku, a black *kasuri* kimono tied with a white *heko obi* sash, and bootees. His eyes are swollen as if he had just been sobbing, frightened of being photographed alone. After being coddled and comforted, he had ceased crying long enough for the photographer to quickly press the shutter.

I have only scattered memories of Hideo from the time he entered primary school. I only remember him as usually naughty and mischievous, a rascal who never tired of teasing me.

Hideo was born in Sarugaku-chō, Kanda, and I in Nando-chō. About the houses where we lived, I can remember only from the time we moved into our newly built house in Imazato-chō, Shirokane, Shiba (now Minato ward), in 1909.

In those days Imazato-chō was a quiet, residential area with fields, empty lots, and rice paddies within fifty to sixty metres' walk from our house. Built on a corner lot, our new, single-storey Japanese house was large, with eight-mat rooms, one Western-style sitting room and a kitchen.

Perhaps because of its size, and the fact that we were a family of only four and a maid, others often came to live with us. My mother's youngest brother, Saburō, who carried on father's work, had earlier come at the age of twelve or thirteen from Kyoto to live with us. He was then commuting to the Industrial Arts School, now Tokyo Metropolitan Industrial High School. Saburō was fifteen years younger than our mother and small in stature, so we called him Little Uncle, but he seemed a brother to us. We also had some boarders, two Keiō University students who were sons of relatives of Kōkichi Mikimoto, the founder of Japan's famous cultured pearls, and the daughter of an acquaintance attending Women's Medical School.

Having been appointed factory head at Mikimoto Pearl and Precious Metals, father was later handpicked by Mikimoto for his second trip abroad to study jewellery accessory factories, and became the first person in Japan to learn diamond-cutting techniques. In gratitude for this, our father always saw that we cared for Mikimoto's relatives. In this respect, Hideo like his father never forgot past favours.

Not only was our house big, the main yard, too, was spacious. Father, Saburō and Hideo used to put up a net and play tennis in the yard. Around 1965, however, when Hideo visited the site of the Shirokane house in Imazato-chō, he remarked the yard didn't seem as big as before. Perhaps we saw it through the eyes of little children.

Outside the living room veranda, father made a gourd-shaped cement pond. He placed carp and goldfish in it, and to one side planted a weeping maple tree, the "red hanging" type. The young red leaves showed their crimson beauty more than in early spring when the leaves sprouted red.

Father, who loved greenery, planted a variety of trees in the main yard. There were other maples that blossomed into colour in autumn, a silver fragrant olive tree, a golden fragrant olive tree, a white plum tree, a red plum tree, two or three varieties of camellias and some sacred bamboos. In front of these were numerous flowers: Japanese laurel, chloranthus, spear flowers, azaleas, magnolias, white lotuses, cotton roses, hydrangeas, Japanese sunflowers, spiraceas, etc. One corner had an empress tree with a big trunk and a banana tree with big leaves. In addition, father would so often purchase saplings and plants that when he returned from occasional outings with Hideo on festival days, our mother would complain.

The backyard had a white fig tree that bore its annual sweet figs, a pomegranate and an astringent persimmon; there was also an apple tree that bore small inedible apples, and tear grass with a hard seed I often used to play house with.

The Latin for tear grass, *lacruma-job*, means "Job's tears". Job, of course, appears in the Old Testament, and though a man of deep faith and righteousness, he was afflicted with a disease so dreadful that his wife disowned him. He suffered unbearable hardships without ever losing his faith.

"Job's tears" was not responsible, but the Shirokane house was marked by dark memories of illness or misfortune.

Within a year of our moving there, our father's foster mother, who was then living with us, was found dead in the bathroom. Also, during the ten years that Hideo attended primary and middle schools, my mother's health remained frail. Then one misfortune followed another: father died, the same year mother came down with haemoptysis, and Hideo fell critically ill. Then the Great Kantō Earthquake struck while mother was convalescing in Kamakura.

The earthquake had neither burnt nor destroyed the Shirokane house, but had tilted it. We lived in this tilted house until debts forced us to sell it. It required repairs to the foundations before the sale. The buyer, a treacherous fellow, made the first payment, but reneged on the second and third payments that had been agreed upon. My mother and Uncle Saburō went repeatedly to collect, but to no avail, and finally we had to bear our fate silently.

In a newspaper article, the following reminiscences of Mitsumasa [Kume] Nomura, President of the Hotel New Grand in Yokohama and Hideo's golfing companion in those years, are recorded: "Since childhood, Hide-chan was full of curiosity and argumentative in personality."

Mitsumasa was the youngest brother of the two Keio University students who were the relatives of Mikimoto boarding at our Shirokane house. He often came to be with his brothers and to play with us, though he himself never lived with us. He was three years older than Hideo, and made a good playmate for him.

Since their hometown was on Tatoku Island in the beautiful waters of Ago Bay in Shima, Mie prefecture, the home of Mikimoto cultured pearls, Hideo and I went to stay there during the summer. Because I went with my mother, I stayed two or three days at most; but Hideo stayed up to ten or fifteen days, swimming all day with Mitsumasa, getting a dark suntan.

Hideo apparently often used to drill Mitsumasa with questions. Once he asked, "Why do trains run?" Mitsumasa gave a simple reply, but Hideo persisted with "Why?" and "For what reasons?"

On the other hand, Hideo had a mischievous trait. A relative's grandmother had visited from the countryside to spend a night or two. Hideo connived with Mitsumasa, saying, "Let's scare her", and proceeded to rub candle wax on the veranda. When the grandmother left the room she lost her footing, slipped and fell on her buttocks; the boys watching from hiding places giggled in great humour.

Mitsumasa Nomura adds, "Nonetheless, Hideo was a son who cared about his mother."

I was at a loss how Nomura could call Hideo, then a child, a son who cared, when suddenly I remembered reading a newspaper article in 1975 that perhaps gave a clue.

From our house, Hideo and I used to walk some ten minutes to Shirokane Primary School in Minato ward. In 1975, when the school was celebrating its one-hundredth anniversary, former classmates and I had made donations. A memorial celebration had been held at Happō-en, and the Memorial Archive Exhibition was open to the public at the school.

The Archive Exhibition included two items discovered in a safe after some sixty years: Jirō Osaragi's speech presented at the 1912 graduation ceremony, and Hideo's second-grade composition written at the age of seven.

The author Jirō Osaragi graduated in March 1912, and his reply speech as class representative had been skilfully written in brush on Japanese *washi* paper:

> Our school has kindly prepared for us this graduation ceremony. The principal has kindly provided us with instructions, and it is the greatest honour for us pupils to offer him our most esteemed appreciation.

It is signed "Graduating Class Representative Kiyohiko Nojiri" (Jirō Osaragi's real name).

Both the speech and Hideo's composition were bound in the booklet "Annual Best Compositions: School Year 1910", a collection written by pupils from second through sixth grades. It has survived since Shirokane Primary School escaped destruction both during the Great Kantō Earthquake and World War II.

Hideo must have been surprised to hear about this and to be reminded about the primary school he had walked to as a child. With face aglow, he said: "If I wrote that in second grade, it's probably my first composition." Then he took a brush and wrote on a poetry card "Writing criticism is to attain the path to non-self", and sent it to commemorate the one-hundredth anniversary of the school.

A photograph showing Hideo's composition and Osaragi's speech in response appeared with the article in the *Yomiuri Newspaper* of 14 November 1975.

The first two lines of the composition are underlined and the last three double underlined:

Obligations To My Parents

The clothes I wear, my mother sewed for me. I am able to attend school, thanks to father and mother. At home, they care for me. I must never forget their love. To return their love, I must obey father and mother, not worry them, and listen to my teachers' instructions at school. In this way, I will repay my parents.

A Second Grader, Hideo Kobayashi

After it, the teacher comments: "Yes, not worrying your parents is best. How good you are with words."

This love for his parents expressed with resolve in Hideo's first composition evidently showed in his early boyhood. For this reason, Nomura said that Hideo's love for his parents continued into his adulthood. To others he may have appeared quite irresponsible to his mother. I too felt that he was quite irresponsible in his higher school and college days. But he did care about his mother. Many close friends also have avowed that few were as filial as he.

Three years had passed since our father's death. Mother returned to Tokyo from Kamakura, where she had recuperated, then the three of us moved to the rented house in Mabashi, Kōenji. My mother's shoulders were always stiff and our chore since childhood had been to massage them. Some five months after moving to Mabashi, however, Hideo began the coterie magazine *Seidō Jidai* (The Age of Bronze), which made him more irresponsible at home; he spent little time at home and left all the massaging to me. I too became busy attending Tokyo Women's College, and wanted any spare time for my studies. I resented the massaging and fumed inside as I massaged our mother's bony shoulders. Mother probably sensed this. She scolded me, "You're not very conscientious. Your brother is far more serious about it." Her words gave me a jolt.

Had I heard right—that Hideo was conscientious? It was he who was running footloose, causing her to worry unduly. I was the one earnestly caring for her. If she didn't recognize this, I would cease listening to her and stop massaging her. These words came to my lips but I swallowed them, shedding bitter tears.

However, some years later as I came to know what Hideo had gone through, I understood my mother's words. By conscientious and unconscientious she had meant sincerity and insincerity. Although I, a serious student, had obeyed my mother, I was filled with selfishness and bitter complaints; I was not genuinely sincere with others. My mother knew this well. Hideo possessed that crucial trait of sincerity, though his life may have seemed unconscientious.

With her meaning of sincerity in mind, I re-read with more care that second-grade composition and smiled sardonically, sensing that sincerity typical of Hideo.

The last line—"I will repay my parents"—expressed with resolve and confidence, seemed so much like him. Hideo's aphoristic or, negatively put, dogmatic style already showed in this childhood composition.

As the article appeared in bold headline — "Hideo Kobayashi's Composition and Jirō Osaragi's Speech: Geniuses Budding in Early Childhood" —Hideo's childhood composition was a harbinger of his individuality.

Hideo himself once said to me,

> Individuality is endowed by Heaven. It is a gift. Though immature, though crude, an endowed fellow will show a "gleam" of it. All babies have it. However, the "gleam" alone is not individuality. Only a person tempered in society develops individuality.

For twenty and even thirty years following the writing of this composition, Hideo confronted problems in society, each having to be overcome, all the while tempering and moulding his individuality.

Chapter 4
My Brother, The Rascal

From the end of the Meiji period to the early Taishō Period in 1912, most Japanese families were still steeped in feudalism, and the motto "Men are above women" tended to limit education for girls. However, my mother's father was a scholar who instructed Michitaka Kujō at the Kujō family residence.* He insisted that all his children be well educated from an early age. This included my mother, Seiko Jōya, who graduated from a girls' school and had all the proper training for a girl of those times.

She was adept as a seamstress and qualified as a tea-ceremony and flower-arrangement instructor. She could knit, make paste-up doll pictures and artificial flowers. Her ability on the *koto* qualified her as an instructor in the Yamada School. Since she enjoyed playing the *koto*, she taught me when I entered first grade.

But mother did not appear particularly happy with her marriage. Father, with his artisan spirit, devoted his time to work, leaving all the family affairs to our mother. This left her alone at home, but she remained a dutiful mistress of the household. She obeyed her mother-in-law, our father's foster mother, then attended to father. She spent her days sewing or washing, starching, and re-sewing kimonos. Not once did I see her enjoying her hobbies, such as knitting or making artificial flowers. Even the *koto* that she so enjoyed playing, she only occasionally strummed in secret after putting me to bed, probably to escape the critical eyes of her mother-in-law and father. I used to fall asleep to her playing such tunes as "Pine Trees with Roots" or "Sarashi" as if listening to bedtime lullabies. Her only real pleasure came once a month, when she went to a kabuki play, but she indulged only when father had gone elsewhere.

My mother was also frail. Although she was taking traditional decocted medicine, I was shocked one day when I saw her gulping down fresh, terrapin blood.

---

* Writings claim that it was the great-grandfather, not the grandfather, who was the tutor to Michitaka Kujō, father of Empress Teimei, wife of the Taishō Emperor.

To the Shirokane house, the grocer, the liquor store man, the butcher and others made deliveries almost daily. A high-spirited fishmonger came too, shouldering a balancing scale. He often came around to the back, entered through the kitchen door, scooped up some water from the kitchen sink and scaled the fish, which he then sliced in front of us. I used to watch, fascinated. One day he brought in a terrapin, which my mother had ordered, explaining that she was to drink its blood. Frightened, I ran off without seeing how he drained the blood, then in trepidation made my way back. I saw her drinking the fresh blood from a teacup in one gulp; she grimaced as if it were poison.

Our family was so old-fashioned that I was the victim of female discrimination. Hideo was the eldest son who was to inherit the family name. I was the younger child and a girl, which severely limited my activities. Whenever I tried to follow Hideo out of the house, mother would stop me, saying I was too little or such places were not for girls. When I tried to join Hideo in an activity at home, mother would reprimand me, saying that I was behaving improperly as a girl.

Hideo was sent to a kindergarten, whereas I was not. Nonetheless, by watching Hideo, I managed to learn some simple arithmetic and the *katakana* alphabet before entering primary school. In those days lessons began with *katakana*.

Dissatisfied at not being treated equally, I constantly fought with Hideo. On every matter, I turned on him—though I knew I could not defeat him. I struck out blindly since I was unable to out-argue him. He would simply trip and toss me; then I would scream, blow my nose hard and start sobbing.

In fun, Hideo nicknamed me "Gramophone", yelling, "Hey, Gramophone, here Gramophone!"

Losing my temper I would grapple with him again, and Hideo would send me sprawling. "Now, I'm going to turn the handle," he would tease, turning his arm in exaggerated circular motion. In those days the box-shaped gramophone had a large horn fixed to it, and the handle had to be turned to play the record.

I would grow angrier and begin to wail, only to succumb to his ploy. Even more elated now he would continue to tease: "Now, now the gramophone's about to play again." I would burst out crying, blowing my nose and sobbing. My mother and Uncle Saburō would stand by giggling, and my sobbing would go on and on.

"It's your fault, because you cry," mother would scold me. This would upset me even more. I would run out to the end of the hallway, bursting into tears again. I remember once inscribing on the wall there "You are a mean brother" in small pencilled letters.

As for the gramophone, we often played it when we were small, although, of course, it was not intended for us children. Before I was born, my father was sent by the Ministry of Education to investigate the precious metal industries in America and Europe, then again after we had moved to Shirokane. On such occasions he probably purchased records abroad. We had numerous opera records, which, I later learned, included *Faust*, *Tosca*, *Lohengrin*, and *La Bohème*. Hideo did not fully understand them, but he knew how to operate the gramophone. Our father, while drinking beer at suppertime, often used to direct Hideo, who had finished eating, to play a record for him.

"That song expresses the joy of having received a jewel," my father would explain to Hideo.

We had other smaller records of Japanese *naniwabushi* folk songs, which my father sometimes hummed to. He appeared to have liked music. We had another older gramophone, which required a cylindrical record. Hideo often brought this out and listened to records whose titles I have no knowledge of.

Father used opera records, though undoubtedly recordings of famous Western singers, and his *naniwabushi* records, for experiments. Father's most noted work, however, was techniques for polishing diamonds that he had imported to Japan. Hideo used to say, however, that father's craze to make or invent new things had brought numerous other patents to his name. After grandmother died in 1910, he hauled machines, tools and metal sheets into her small room. Using the room as a workshop, he tirelessly made one item after another. I remember the tortoise-shell combs and hair bands, copper saucers, material to polish brass and other metals, lying about the house. Hideo too used to enter the workshop room, apparently to try his hand at making things.

My father became the first in Japan to create a ruby gramophone needle. He would get Hideo to start the record to test his newly created needle, and would say, "It won't do; let's redo it," if he heard the slightest scratching or screeching. Then he would patiently rethink and remake the needle, repeatedly testing by trial and error. Each time, Hideo operated the gramophone, playing the needle on the record over and over. Most likely, as a child he felt a part of his father's project of inventing the new needle. Hoping for success, as did his father, he, still a child, tirelessly operated the gramophone.

I believe Hideo inherited all of father's traits: feeling the excruciating effort in inventing even a small item, while enjoying every moment of the struggle. Hideo had probably gained an appreciation of music during this time, listening repeatedly to the world's classics.

His passion for research, keen curiosity, bold sense of adventure and unwavering enthusiasm that was just like father's had already revealed itself in Hideo's childhood.

The Shirokane house, exposed to the sunny southside, had a long veranda outside both the eight-mat living room and my mother's six-mat room. Though the one-storey house had gas heaters, the children's room was warmed only by a charcoal brazier, so we often sunned ourselves on this veranda on fine winter days. Whenever we were not bickering, Hideo would bring three tangerines, eating them as we sat side by side, stretching out our legs in the sun on the veranda. After we ate one each, Hideo would peel the third, count the number of tangerine pieces, and hand me half. We both often wore *haori* coats stuffed thick with soft cotton over our kimonos.

I had just started primary school, I believe, when one fine day the quilts were spread out in the sun on the veranda floor, so that only the lower rain-shutter was showing. As if on a balancing beam, Hideo precariously walked on his toes along the edge of the shutter beside the veranda without stepping on the quilts. He had gone back and forth several times, enjoying the thrill, when he suddenly spotted me on top of the quilts watching him.

"Get on. This time I'll walk across with you on my back, Fuji-chan."

"No." I shook my head. "We'll fall."

"Don't worry. We won't fall. You just saw me tiptoe across. We won't fall."

"You will if you carry me," I said.

"Don't worry," Hideo shouted, not accepting a refusal. I was afraid, but I got on nonetheless, as if to join him in the adventure.

Hideo began to tiptoe along the railing, slowly and carefully. I clung to his back, fearing for my life as I pressed my cheek against his thin neck protruding from his kimono collar. With my weight on him, and without the free use of his hands that held me on his back, he wobbled perilously. Taking one step after another along the railing, after not more than five or six steps as my body wavered, he lost his balance and both of us tumbled into the yard.

It didn't hurt, but I was stunned and sobbing when I looked up at Hideo. "I told you we'd fall!" I was about to yell at him. But then Hideo, finally picking himself up, looked at my face and said apologetically with an embarrassed look, "We fell after all." When he grinned, I could not yell at him, get angry or cry. We both burst out laughing.

About the same time, when he was in third grade, father was having Hideo learn an aikidō-type "health exercise". Although he occasionally practised at home, in shorts and naked from the waist up, he went for his lessons I don't know how far. His instructor visited our house only once or twice, and I only remember him surprisingly eating an entire tangerine, peel and all.

Father, proud of Hideo's health exercises, often had him demonstrate when we had guests. In the cold Hideo would strip down to his shorts in the parlour, and then yell out "Ehh-Ehh" as he slammed and pounded on his body. I never knew how good he was, but his fierceness used to impress me as I watched with the guests.

About this time too, the parents whose two sons were boarding with us came to Tokyo to visit at our Shirokane house. The four of them and we, the four members of the Kobayashi family, decided on a day's outing to the ocean, then known as the Morigasaki Coast not far from Ōmori Station.

It must have been early May, too early for the swimming season, since for lunch we had horse beans and green peas mixed in rice that Hideo and I liked.

We went in a rickshaw from the station to the ocean-side inn. Mother held me in her lap in the rickshaw. The two students and Hideo said they wanted to walk, and left before us. I wanted to go with them, but mother held me tight in the rickshaw.

Determined not to be overtaken by the rickshaw, the three boys walked quickly ahead. Between the uniforms of the two students I could see Hideo wearing a navy blue muslin patterned kimono with sleeves tucked in at the shoulders and a Kokura *hakama*, with lace-up shoes. Full of envy, I watched as little Hideo anxiously pursued the uniformed students at full speed, anxious not to be left behind. I momentarily lost sight of them, but stretching my neck to see their position, I saw them reappear far up the road, turn around, and wave their hands at us. They raced on, veering off the road, crossing the fields into the woods, and finding short cuts. It seemed such fun and such an adventure.

Upon arriving at the inn, we had our lunch, rested briefly, and the fathers and the boys went out, perhaps to fish. The mothers relaxed and talked in a room on the second floor.

I was left alone and bored; leaning against the veranda railing upstairs, I looked at the ocean beyond and at the inn garden below. The garden had a big pond with growing reeds, spanned by a bridge in the middle where a boat floated. In it I spotted Hideo, who had just gone off, manoeuvring the boat precariously with its big rudder.

I ran down from the second floor and somehow made it to the garden, and then onto the bridge.

"Hideo, let me on too."

From the boat, he said, "No, stay there. Stop!" At first he refused to let me on.

When I persisted, he grudgingly relented, and brought the boat alongside the bridge. Holding onto the bridge railing, I managed to lower my legs, but was afraid to let go with the boat wobbling so. In the meantime, Hideo began to steer the boat away from the bridge, whereupon I fell straight into the pond. Fortunately, since it was shallow there, my feet touched bottom, with the water reaching up to my neck. I finally crawled onto the bridge where Hideo yelled at me, "How can you get on the boat holding onto the bridge, stupid?"

Thereafter, I only remember running back to the corridor soaked in my muslin kimono to the room where mother was.

Chapter 5
Eyeglasses, Eyeglasses, How Well I Can See!

Some six months after Hideo's death, the moss that Hideo loved covered the bottom of the pagoda-shaped headstone of his grave at Tōkeiji Temple. It flourished perhaps because so many had poured water over the headstone. By summer, after I had visited his grave numerous times, the gravesite reminded me of the graves of the Forty-seven Samurai at Sengakuji Temple.

Our house in Shirokane was located near the Sengakuji Temple, or so it seemed since everyone walked in those days, but by today's standards it was quite a hike. In my primary school days I often accompanied Hideo or Uncle Saburō there, since they frequently took out-of-town relatives to this nearby tourist spot. From fifth grade on it became solely my job instead of Hideo's. I had visited so often that the temple no longer held any interest for me, but I felt an air of importance in taking first-time visitors there.

Those days, perhaps unlike today, crowds of people visited the gravesite of the Forty-seven Samurai at Sengakuji Temple and lit so many incense sticks as offerings that the smoke was said never to dissipate.

Although not to the extent of the smoke that continually hovered over the samurai's graves, the mourners' fresh flowers covered Hideo's gravesite whenever I visited. Haruko and Hideo's wife Kiyomi too remarked how often they saw varieties of fresh flowers that had been placed there. They were so beautiful compared to those I had bought in Tokyo. I was so embarrassed that I brought flowers to his nearby Kamakura home to place before his photo.

I found not only flowers but also a bound booklet filled with *tanka* poems on *washi* paper eulogizing him before the Buddhist hundred-day memorial period had elapsed. Judging from the poems, the writer highly esteemed Hideo and had even met him once. His name and address appeared at the end of the booklet. Also, a pack of Peace cigarettes had been placed there—Hideo's favourites—though they had already been completely soaked in a recent rainfall.

About that time, Kiyomi told me a touching story. At Hideo's grave at Tōkeiji Temple in north Kamakura, a young Yokohama girl and a young

Kyūshū man met quite by coincidence. They had not met before but had a mutual interest, as fervent admirers of Hideo Kobayashi, in visiting the grave. After offering their prayers, they decided to walk to Hideo's house of thirty years on a nearby low-lying mountain behind Hachiman Shrine. At that time, however, the house was owned by Hideo's friend, Chōzō Yoshii of the Yoshii Gallery, where I had visited numerous times. It commanded a breath-taking view, but the walk up, which took half an hour from the station, always required a rest.

The young people found only Mr Yoshii's mother at home, but she welcomed them in. Just being shown the garden gave the two much satisfaction as they bade her farewell. No doubt they would have had a last look at the front gate several times as they descended.

They found Hideo's Swedish prefab house where he lived his last eight years. They tried to enter but a barking dog prevented them, forcing them to retrace their steps. Heading towards Kamakura station, they dropped in at the Ōshige Sushi Restaurant, one of Hideo's favourites, where they had sushi, then parted.

Mr Yoshii's mother received a polite letter of thanks from both of them, I heard. No one knows what the new acquaintances had thought or discussed about Hideo, nor do I care.

This girl also sent me a note soon after. It was a picture postcard mailed about the end of April, some two months after the First Year Memorial of Hideo's death, from Kiyoharu in Yamanashi prefecture. The card explained that the young man she met was a pre-med student, whose hospitalized mother had died of cancer at the end of the previous year and who believed, as did Hideo Kobayashi, that his mother had been reincarnated as a firefly. As for herself, she intended from that year to visit each year the dozen or so cherry-blossom sites Kobayashi had visited in Japan.

I also heard that many visitors came to Kamanta Inn in Oku-Yugawara town, Izu Peninsula, asking for the room Hideo had stayed in so they could spend the night there. From this, I can imagine also the numbers of guests coming to stay at Tamanoyu Inn at Yufuin town, Ōita prefecture, another of Hideo's favourites in his later years.

Hideo was very fond of sushi, particularly young punctatus *shinko* sushi that could only be had from late summer to early fall. During this short season, Hideo ate them almost daily at Ōshige Sushi Restaurant. This year again in the same season, I heard that the master of Ōshige Sushi Restaurant, in remembrance of Hideo, had delivered some young punctatus sushi to place before his photograph.

My brother had this uncanny appeal. Even after his death over and over again I have heard something new about him from sources outside the family, like the endless incense smoke rising at Sengakuji Temple. Each time, I wish that he could have lived longer.

Feeling this way about Hideo's death, I reminisced about my father. After some reading, I came to realize the stature my father had.

Uncle Saburō, who had carried on the Japan Diamond Corporation founded by my father, once explained that he was not much of a family man, but he looked after people, and was unusually diligent regarding his work. Father, who had once studied pedagogy, instructed Uncle Saburō and numerous others at great length about the skills and knowledge that he painstakingly learned abroad and introduced to Japan, not keeping such skills solely to himself.

Sent abroad for the first time in 1903 by the Ministry of Education, he returned after observing and studying the precious metal skills and techniques in the industrial West, but saw the need for the Ministry of Education to establish a school to teach these techniques in Japan. Acceding to his request, the Ministry of Education founded the Tokyo Higher School of Technology. To this newly founded technical school, my father had Uncle Saburō transfer from Kaisei Middle School to learn basic metallurgy techniques.

I was overjoyed to learn that, throughout, my father had been true to his fellow workers and to his work, traits Hideo shared.

It was about three years ago. I had been embarrassed and careless when a man who had high regard for my father's work requested my father's birth date in order to write an article about him in the magazine *Hōseki to Kikinzoku Kōgei* (Techniques of Jewellery and Precious Metals). Not remembering, I went to Hideo, but of course he too had forgotten. Knowing Minato Ward Office had it in the family register but not knowing the location of the Office, I let the days go by, regretting the delay with it on my mind. Finally I forgot.

Hideo died and I began to remember about my father. I recalled this incident a year later when I asked publishers of Shinchōsha and Haruko to help trace my father's birth date. Though too late for the article, I decided to inform the man, but had lost his address. He had sent me two copies of the magazine, but these I had given away. Remembering a New Year's card from him, I frantically looked in the drawer, finding there a pack of New Year's cards, one with his address. I answered him with an apology. He wrote a few days later, thanking me deeply, saying that this would help him complete a history on Mikimoto as well. Much relieved, I thought, "never forget a promise", no matter how belated.

The above story may have nothing to do with Hideo directly, but our father's birthday had a certain significance for Hideo, which is why I was surprised when I learned it.

Hideo and I each had two dates of birth—the actual dates we were born and the dates on which we were registered, probably a few days after birth. Not being much of a family man, our father probably did not register our birth dates immediately, nor could our mother, being too weak to do so after giving birth.

The family register shows that I was born on 3 June; however, both my mother and Aunt Yūko Jōya and I believed that 19 May is the real date. On 19 May I celebrate my birthday among family members and close friends, and receive gifts, preferring the month of May to June, and the May birthstone of emerald to the June birthstone of pearl. But I use the June date on official documents and tax declarations. The register shows 11 April as Hideo's birth date, but I heard from Aunt Yūko Jōya the actual date to be near the end of March. I believe this to be correct, since she has a good memory for dates. I forget the exact date since no one is alive anymore to verify it.

Hideo was not concerned about his own birthday, so either date was good enough for him. My father's birth date, however, gave me a shock. My father's registered birth date, though unlikely to be the actual one, falls on 27 March 1879. Hideo was presumably born at the end of March so it was possible that it fell on the same date, the 27th, as father's. As diviners do by reading palms and body features, I believe one can predict personality traits by birth dates, so Hideo's traits resembled father's not only in that they were father and son, but possibly by their almost identical birth dates. Though this sounds incredible, some even say that blood type can reveal one's personality traits.

One Hideo Kobayashi admirer once asked me, "What is Mr Kobayashi's blood type?" Being forgetful and not knowing even my own blood type, I had to ask Hideo's daughter Haruko. She replied that it was type B.*

When I was a small girl, my mother often scolded me, but not Hideo. When we fought, I was blamed though I considered Hideo to be at fault. For this unfair treatment, I continued to hold a grudge against Hideo; yet I can never forget one time when my mother lashed out at Hideo.

It happened when Hideo was probably still a first-grader and I had yet to enter primary school. Uncle Saburō was attending Kaisei Middle School. Around then Uncle Saburō and Hideo began to grapple and scuffle with a young girl, a medical student boarder at our house. They finally managed to pull her down and jump onto her, shouting. I wanted to join in, but just stood to one side watching, as her kimono parted and exposed her white legs to her thighs. She giggled in fun. Just then, mother appeared with a demon-

---

* It is believed in Japan that people of blood type B tend to be insensitive, to conduct themselves as they please and to have strong personalities. They are often regarded as eccentric, free-spirited and contented with themselves.

like look on her face, and screamed at Uncle Saburō and Hideo. Though Uncle Saburō and Hideo had got to their feet and had grown quiet, mother's barrage continued so fiercely I was shocked. Why had she scolded them when they were just having some fun? Shouldn't she rather have scolded Hideo more for fighting me?

After I entered primary school, I started to imitate Hideo. Though he was a despicable rascal, I respected him after hearing how he ranked top in his class and his teacher had praised him for his writing ability. So in every way, I tried to imitate him. Hideo was an avid reader, so I often read. From fifth grade he edited a class periodical, so I edited a booklet, "Girls' Time", with another girl. Ours was not circulated as a class periodical, but still we enjoyed reading it to each other. We served both as writers and readers.

From fifth grade, Hideo's class teacher was Mr Ozawa whose skilful teaching methods were highly regarded by the school. He had organized summer school camps, which, though small in scale, were innovative for those years. A photograph taken one summer in Hideo's fifth or sixth grade shows Mr Ozawa and another leader with ten or so bare-chested boys posing at the beach about to go swimming perhaps. The pupils have on baggy swimming drawers or loincloths. Hideo in striped, baggy drawers, appears quite manly, his legs set firmly apart.

Mr Ozawa gave Hideo a pen-name at his graduation. He apparently did so should Hideo become a writer someday, but Hideo never used it and forgot the name.

I envied Hideo for having a pen-name, so I imitated him. When I became a fifth-grader I chose the best, thickest notebook, which I had received as a gift, and put on its cover "Composition Practice Book". Then I began to write. I had my class teacher read and evaluate each composition, and by the summer of my sixth grade I had completed about fifty.

My fifth- and sixth-grade class teacher was a thin, middle-aged woman with a broad forehead who, though pale and always coughing, read my compositions without showing the slightest displeasure. Late into the evening, always coughing, she would also conscientiously help me with my entrance exam studies for girls' middle school. After I graduated, she retired and kept herself in seclusion at home. Though I tried to see her once with a friend, she had already become bed-ridden. A year later, she passed away. She was not a friendly teacher but was a truly dedicated one.

The "Composition Practice Book" became a secret between us. Finally I asked her for a pen-name, and to select the best composition. She gave me the pen-name "Kiyoka" and chose as the best composition "Hatsuchigo" (First Hairdo)—a non-existent word. I had made up the title by attaching the first half of the word *hatsushimada*, that I happened to see somewhere, to the second half of the word *ochigo* (a Japanese hairdo).

Around that time, a hairdresser came to the house once a week or every five days to set my mother's hair in *marumage* style. During the New Year's vacation when I was in fifth grade, my mother and the hairdresser suggested the *ochigo* hairdo, which Ushiwakamaru (the childhood name of the hero Yoshitsune) wore, for me.

Gathered at the top of the head, my hair was divided into two, then dampened with hair oil and set by *kondosa* black paper at the back in the form of two rings. Few children those days enjoyed this style, the hair being raised high and weighing so much as to make the head uncomfortable.

I felt self-conscious, but I was elated after my mother, the hairdresser and the maid all commented on how cute I looked.

My composition "Hatsuchigo" described this hairdo: my no longer feeling like a fifth-grader, the heaviness of my head, the remarks on how cute I looked, my feeling too self-conscious to go outside, and Hideo staring at me in astonishment. But I did not write about the misery that followed.

Hideo had stared big-eyed at me and jeered, "Hey, hey, Eyeglasses, Eyeglasses!" peering through his thumbs and fingers which he held up like a pair of eyeglasses. Angry, I chased him, but he suddenly disappeared. Then he reappeared and started hooting at me, "Eyeglasses, Eyeglasses, how well I can see!"

Uncle Saburō was entering the house when Hideo yelled out so Uncle Saburō could hear "Eyeglasses, Eyeglasses!" Uncle Saburō too couldn't help staring at my hair and yelling out, "Hey, Eyeglasses", bursting into laughter.

I was boiling with anger. Moreover, my head grew heavy and began to hurt, the hair being stretched so tight. That night I asked my mother to undo the *ochigo* hairdo, which had been so neatly made up.

However spiteful he was then, I came to love writing no matter how imperfect my writing was, because I had Hideo to imitate, and I now remain ever thankful to him.

Chapter 6
Wide Random Reading Develops
A Flexibility—Apt To Be Lost In Man

Those days we used to hear almost daily the carefree calls of street vendors and the sound of their bells and horns as they walked by.

Spring brought vendors selling seedlings. Then summer saw vendors selling wind chimes sounding ring-a-ding-ding; a goldfish vendor, passing by shouting energetically; a medicine vendor shouldering a tiered-drawer box, ringing loudly, striking the metal knobs of the drawers. He was said to be a pharmacist selling *jōsai*, a medical concoction for heat fatigue. Also a horn-blowing bean curd vendor and a bell-ringing boiled-bean vendor passed by early in the morning. Hearing his bell in the morning, Hideo and I used to dash out of the house holding two copper *sen* coins to buy boiled soybeans or some kidney beans for our school lunches.

In winter, in particular we eagerly awaited the hot roast-bean vendor; the winters in Tokyo in those days were colder than today. Also, perhaps because of the inadequacy of the heating at home, we used to wear *haori* coats over thick, cotton-padded kimonos and flannel tights, which came down to our ankles. Ashamed of long drawers showing below our kimono hems, Hideo and I used to roll up our tights, which then exposed our bare legs between our *tabi* socks and kimono. I remember the bared portion chapping and hurting painfully whenever we took a steaming hot bath.

At that time, many winter days saw dry winds that pierced right through our bodies; the sky would grow overcast and grey, with clouds threatening snow. On such dreary days, the roast soybean vendor came calling, "Hot roast beans, steaming roast beans hot from the pan!" as he pulled his cart. When Hideo heard the call, he would throw down his books, leap up from the *kotatsu* table, and get two *sen* coins from Mother doing needlework nearby. Then, yelling "Bean man!" he would dash outside. I, in pursuit, would jump from the *kotatsu* table, though I realized that remaining there would be warmer.

Sounding a last lusty call, "Steaming hot roast beans!" the bean vendor with his head wrapped in a handkerchief would stop his cart before our house. Then he roasted the beans inside the box-like wire mesh that hung above, and shook it over the charcoal fire glowing in his cart. Inside the wire mesh, the beans would begin to crackle.

Waiting for the beans to roast, Hideo and I shrank our necks further down into our kimonos and stamped our feet to keep warm. Then the vendor would fill the hot beans, dried red beans that had been soaked in water and sprinkled with salt, in one heap inside a triangular fold of newspaper. With our beans we ran back inside the house, sat snugly at the warm *kotatsu* table, and munched on the hot beans, picking them out of the bag. Those hot beans were a treat for children then, fancy Western sweets being mostly unavailable in Japan.

On such occasions, Hideo and I felt particularly close. Another fond memory came from going to see the "chrysanthemum dolls", followed by a movie. Since this was once a year, we went a total of perhaps three or four times. In those days, between October and November chrysanthemum dolls were exhibited at the large Ryōgoku National Arena, though such exhibitions are still held in places today on a smaller scale. The exhibits displayed scenes from kabuki plays such as *Chūshingura* (The Treasury of Loyal Retainers) and *Sukeroku*, and modern plays such as *Hototogisu* (Cuckoo) and *Konjikiyasha* (The Demon Gold), with dolls resembling the performers' faces and their costumes decorated with chrysanthemum flowers. For children they included scenes from plays such as *Hanasaka Jijii* (Old Man Hanasaku), *Urashima Tarō* and *Kachikachi Yama* (Mount Kachikachi), which Hideo and I took in one at a time in great delight. We enjoyed especially the doll's face of Urashima Tarō changing into an old man's as he opened the small treasure chest.

That autumn day was a gala outing for the four of us—Mother, the maid, Hideo and I. After seeing the chrysanthemum dolls, we would go to Asakusa for a movie, so Hideo and I left home with our hearts full of anticipation. Then too we would ride the now defunct clanging trolley car, and change trolleys before reaching Ryōgoku. Since a trolley ride was rare, Hideo and I would head straight to the front without sitting and stand all the way watching the Tokyo street scenes.

After seeing the chrysanthemum-doll exhibits, we came out to a wider area. A guide stood beside a stage explaining the setting there, as the characters in the play were dolls that were unable to talk. The stage was called a "seven-change stage" (sometimes a five-change stage was used), whose settings changed seven times. There was no lowering of the curtain as the electrically operated props changed instantaneously. We watched excitedly as the backdrop wall fell, another popped up from the scene behind, a house appeared from below, some items disappeared on both sides and were replaced by others.

Following this, we went to Asakusa for lunch, our second treat of the day. It was Hideo who decided on the lunch for us but I could only think of an *okame* bowl of buckwheat noodles. Then Hideo gave our mother our orders, but her budget usually allowed us either sushi, fried lobster on a bowl of rice, or buckwheat noodles.

Hideo also agreed to select the movie to see. Twice he would go up and down Asakusa's famous movie row, looking at the large billboards above the theatres before deciding. Whether or not my mother enjoyed it or I understood, we abided by his decision. I remember seeing the Western movies *Anthony and Cleopatra* and *The Cursed Demon*.

Mr Ozawa was Hideo's best teacher in his last two years at primary school; he tried to instil a broad knowledge into his pupils. When Hideo was in sixth grade, Mr Ozawa brought about ten pupils to our house one summer night for my father to speak to them about his trip to Europe and America. The pupils all listened, sitting on the *tatami* mat, and I listened too from the dark veranda—though I forget what he talked about.

The First World War had just broken out in July 1914. I remember Hideo, a sixth-grader, giving a talk in the autumn school assembly on the causes and conditions of the war. It was captivating in presentation and content. I was deeply impressed, but, thinking back now, the speech should be half credited to Mr Ozawa.

In those days, the First Middle School (now Hibiya High School) ranked highest in Japan among middle schools, and any primary school able to place two to three pupils there achieved instant fame. Mr Ozawa's class alone placed seven pupils, which included Hideo. Shirokane Primary School was undoubtedly pleased, but more so was Mr Ozawa.

A large photo shows him with these seven pupils clad in their First Middle School uniforms. Hideo looks proud in a school uniform for the first time, which, intended for two or three years' wear, is too big for him. The collar rises up to his chin with the sleeves hanging over his thumbs.

A gift of providence had provided Hideo in his primary school days with such a teacher as Mr Ozawa, I believe.

Though top of his class in primary school, once Hideo entered middle school, his grades fell to mediocre and then below average. This was natural perhaps, in competing now with Japan's brightest pupils, but Hideo's rebelliousness was a contributing factor. Even back in 1915, the First Middle School, being the route to First Higher School and finally to Tokyo Imperial University, concentrated on studies leading to passing examinations to these schools. It slighted subjects such as literature, music, and P.E., which were not examined. Strict teachers who found novels, music scores or a baseball in a student's briefcase often reprimanded the students and confiscated the items.

Hideo, holding many interests, rebelled against this distorted type of education. In primary school under Mr Ozawa, Hideo had put together magazines to circulate among his classmates, and he continued to read literary works even after entering the First Middle School. Also, every Saturday after school, he went to Hibiya Park Amphitheatre to hear popular military bands play. In time he started to study the mandolin on his own. He also went to the Yoyogi Field to play baseball.

Regardless of this resistance, I felt that Hideo was becoming more like a proper brother from his last year in middle school. That is, I got him to instruct me more than I imitated him. He had helped me to pass the exams for Third Girls' Middle School. He helped me in all the subjects —mathematics, Japanese language and English.

In his last year in middle school, Hideo developed pimples on his face. Irritated by this, he used to rub a pink cream on his face daily. Still, I used to place my English textbook before him, which he peered at while rubbing his face. The cream droplets, which were now dirty, fell onto the pages. Oblivious to this he earnestly explained. If I failed to understand, he lost his temper, but would then resume his explanation with care.

This tendency to explode at me remained with Hideo into his adulthood, particularly regarding my knowledge of words, which fell far short of his. I still know little, but I knew even less over twenty years ago.

At the mountain-top house, on one occasion Hideo was eagerly explaining to me about the nineteenth-century samurai activist Shōin Yoshida about whom Jirō Osaragi, still active then, was writing in the *Asahi Newspaper*. According to Hideo, Shōin had resigned himself to die during his imprisonment, and wrote *Rukonroku* (Records of an Enduring Spirit), leaving with a samurai one copy which was later lost, and the other for safekeeping with a hardened prisoner, which has survived. Having no idea of the contents of the *Records*, the prisoner hid this on him to the end, true to Shōin's request, and thanks to him, we can read the *Records* today.

Hideo explained, "This prisoner entrusted with the *Records* was sent to *entō*." I was unfamiliar with this word.

I inquired, "What does *entō* mean?"

Exasperated, Hideo shouted in amazement, "Your vocabulary is hopeless!"

Then he continued, "It means sentenced to live on an isolated island." Seeing my embarrassment, he comforted me, saying, "But there's no need to become a know-it-all."

I was again embarrassed on another occasion. He had displayed on the drawing-room shelf two large, old pieces of pottery. One was a white Yi Dynasty pot from Korea, and the other a coarse brown tea-pot about thirty centimetres high. I had previously seen this in a photograph with an explanatory note, which I thought read Shinraku pottery.

I inquired, "What does Shinraku mean?"

He lashed out, "What fool would read it Shinraku!" Then he explained. "It reads Shigaraki, a region in Shiga prefecture which has had baked pottery since the Tempyō Period [729–749]. It means that it is one of the oldest fired-pottery sites in Japan."

The same year that Hideo graduated from the First Middle School, he failed the entrance exams to the First Higher School, and had to spend one more year in preparation. Though I had been deeply indebted to him for instructing me, I was unsympathetic when I heard he had failed and ridiculed him harshly using words I have forgotten. I was prepared for his usual counterattack, but he unexpectedly placed his head on his desk as if to hide his face and began sobbing. I was taken aback. I regretted my harshness, but I was at a loss what to do.

Nonetheless, Hideo's rebelling for five years against the middle-school education and an additional year spent as a prep student, I believe, enriched him in no small way in the years that followed.

Until then, our family enjoyed a relatively peaceful, fortunate life, but the following year our father's sudden death changed our lives radically. Since my mother and Uncle Saburō hid financial matters from me, I was not particularly disturbed about it, but Hideo, having been informed as the eldest son, apparently was deeply worried, far more than I.

Soon after my father's death, Mother fell ill. She required complete rest so we had a nurse stay at the Shirokane house. I didn't know the extent to which Hideo was providing for our livelihood, but in higher school Hideo read voraciously book after book. He would start reading five or six books at a time, at home, in the train, and at school. He never ceased reading.

Much later, he commented on this habit: "Wide random reading develops flexibility—apt to be lost in man."

Also, though briefly, Hideo used to go out at nights after supper holding a book and wearing a *hakama* skirt. The book was the New Testament, which he apparently was studying in a Bible Study group at a church in the vicinity. Whether he went on his own or at a friend's invitation, I never found out; but the Bible I knew came from my father's bookcase. Since our household was Buddhist and we had no Christian relatives, why my father had a Bible is unknown to me.

In First Higher School, he resumed playing the mandolin, which he had first begun in the First Middle School. He organized the Crescent Mandolin Club to eventually hold a concert in the Youth Building then at Hongō, Tokyo. I attended with some girl friends to whom I had sold tickets, at Hideo's request to sell some.

Chapter 7
I Cannot Sermonize But Only Confess

As I write about Hideo, I feel burdened when I think back a number of years and realize so clearly how indifferent to everything I had been.

The noted writer Ayako Sono has written: "Faith does not depend upon whether one is an excellent person, but rather on whether one realizes to the core how 'indifferently' he or she has lived."

According to her definition, I certainly am a believer, but may be lacking a faith "to the core".

In our childhood, I admit Hideo angered me with his teasing remarks and loud outbursts, but he never abused me physically. We often fought, but he never angrily hit, bullied or injured me outright. For one to resent a brother, when a child is understandable, but even when I entered college I again grew angry at and hated Hideo for forsaking my mother and me. I did not truly understand, but I believe he has forgiven me. However, indifferent as I was, from my childhood, Hideo stood by me with kindness to the end. He instructed me in so many matters even into our elderly years. Now thinking back, I am filled with regret about my indifference. To his suggestions, advice and warnings, I had just listened "nonchalantly". Out of my stupidity, I did not act on them and this I fully regret.

About this regret, Hideo would probably advise me: "For this reason you'll never, never understand yourself."

In his essay "Watashi no Jinseikan" (My View of Life), Hideo quotes the words of the famous warrior Musashi Miyamoto, "I never regret things", and explains that the writer Kan Kikuchi interprets this to mean: "I regret nothing." But Hideo says it means: "I never regret anything about myself." Hideo says this does not mean that Musashi never regretted anything, because he always acted with great care and propriety. Rather, Hideo thought that self-criticism and the need to settle accounts for past ill deeds were but an artificial veneer, a barrier to understanding one's true self. He warned against the foolhardy self-deception called regret and called upon readers to affirm their past life as unalterable, to hold onto the life one has.

Hideo's interpretation of Musashi holds a vital truth; Hideo himself lived in that spirit, I believe. I, however, cannot lead such a sincere life. So I continue to deceive myself, and am unable to stop my regrets at having wronged Hideo.

Some twenty years ago, I began to lecture in a simple way throughout Japan on the need for the Christian faith, though I believed myself unable to sermonize. Around that time Hideo said: "I cannot sermonize, I can only confess." This jolted me.

I realized that although I had not intended to sermonize, I had been doing this all along. I had been feeling depressed after each lecture. I could not live up to my own words. I was disgusted with my hypocrisy, unable to practise what I was encouraging others to do.

Sermonizing means to stand above others and teach, admonish, guide and advise. I lacked such a high character. Did I not require that instruction? Hideo made me realize this. A lecturer must also be at one with the audience, or humble before the audience. Ever since, I have tried to lecture from my own experiences, making something close to a confession. I owe this to Hideo's few words of advice.

Father's death had left the family without an income and financially dependent on uncles Moku and Saburō and others. Thus when I expressed my desire to enter Tokyo Women's College, my mother and Uncle Saburō opposed it. Instead, my mother, who was still recuperating in Kamakura, and others, had requested Uncle Saburō to arrange a marriage for me without my knowledge. Girls in those days usually married upon graduating from middle school. There was no need for educated girls. Rather than going to college, girls were taught sewing, tea ceremony, and flower arrangement.

I, however, wanted to go to college. I thought that to help support the family, only a college education would assure me of a job with some income. Fortunately, Hideo did not oppose this. This encouraged me all the more to attend Tokyo Women's College. This turned out to be a wise decision. I may have disobeyed my mother, but later my education enabled me to support the family and to develop myself as a person.

As I mentioned before, from childhood I had imitated Hideo in every respect. When Hideo entered the First Higher School and began a coterie magazine and wrote a work of fiction, I too began to write. After I entered college, I completed something resembling a story but, wanting to know its quality, fearfully I asked Hideo to read it. After some time, he finally found time to read it and commented:

> It is not a novel, but a composition. The writing is immature. Also, to write a novel, one must have some memorable experiences. Your lukewarm experiences won't do. You must experience pain and anguish beyond the average person. One must suffer even to the point where one

despairs of mankind. Look at the women writers Fumiko Hayashi and Taiko Hirabayashi for example, how they suffered in their childhood. Such painful experiences can materialize into a novel.

He commented that I lacked the experience for a novel, but did not say that I was hopeless, or that I should cease writing. So, I wrote another story. This time, Hideo made no comment, but he recommended that I go and see some first-rate paintings and sculptures. He suggested the remarkable replicas of Rodin's works at the Tokyo Arts School (now Department of Arts, Tokyo University of Arts) in Ueno. Making up my mind, I went alone and did the best I could to study Rodin's large statues. Impressed and in a state of inexplicable ecstasy, I returned home.

In addition, he explained: "The poems in the classical *Manyōshū* collection are excellent, because the writer is expressing a way of life he believes in. Cherish your experiences, and believe in your way of life."

I had been given this advice, but what was I to do? How could I fully believe in my way of life? Deciding I should read the *Manyō* poems, I purchased a copy of the Iwanami Pocket Book edition, which I began to read but never managed to finish.

In May of 1928, immediately after Hideo left Yasuko, Takamizawa proposed to me. I wrote to Hideo about it, as the only person I could confide in. Receiving Hideo's affirmative reply, I set the marriage date for September, but before then my next story, "Megusuri" (Eye Medicine), was published in the literary magazine *Sōsaku Gekkan* (Creative Writings Monthly) under the name Fujiko Kobayashi. I wrote to Hideo asking for his comments. His reply arrived some months later, after I had already married and become Fujiko Takamizawa. I read his letter with excitement.

(No Date)

Sorry for the delay, since I was wandering about in Kobe.

I read the story. It is skilfully and clearly written. I'll not offer practical criticism for the time being, since I have lost any interest in the subject. As for your style, I'll not mention it either, since I have lost my own "style", but I do notice coarseness in your descriptions. You need to be more elaborate in depicting things. In general, the only method seems to be this: describe quickly both your inner feelings and outer phenomena as accurately and vividly as possible, and then delete what is unnecessary.

The "flavour" of a work is born from strenuous efforts when a writer is young, after one finds a satisfactory form. This effort in the end produces the "fragrance" of the work, and the [word missing in original letter] creates unspeakable charm in places that even the author is unaware of. Your story skilfully depicts, but lacks a certain punch. This is probably because the writer is not quiet inwardly. To write about self-ridicule is most difficult. For self-ridicule to be aesthetic, it must approach insanity. That is, mediocre self-ridicule or self-disgust that is half-hearted cannot move readers; the writer has failed to reach them, because many readers are more capable of laughing at themselves than the writer.

Now, if this were the case, your depicting the heroine becomes a matter of the logic of your consciousness, which means that aesthetic writing relates directly to cultivating a person's character.

Then, if this is a lifetime problem that cannot be resolved except after a lifetime of thought, one is unable to write during one's life. However, an aesthete writes even before resolving this problem, and puts into words the feelings of this or that moment. This is fine.

Then, the problem, ethical to this point, now becomes a problem of aesthetics. Understand this matter well. That is, the feeling of that moment must be transmitted into a fresh image. At this point various problems related to the plastic arts are introduced into literature.

It is very true that the ultimate *raison d'être* for literature is to portray man. Thus, a purely literature-oriented writer like Dostoevsky has no time to take in paintings and music. However, he is a rare genius. It is good to imitate him, but it will be excruciatingly difficult for mediocre people like us. Thus an average writer enlists the aid of painting and music in order to freshen his "image" before writing literature.

You lose out in apparently lacking the culture for the plastic arts and music. So your image tends to become a mere conception.

The other day, I borrowed from Naoya Shiga the works of Kiku Amino, and read her for the first time. Of course, she is not a good writer, but her work is rich in nuances—nuances of temperament. Her collection of novellas, *Mitsuko*, contains a short work titled "Kage" (Shadow), which has something very beautiful about it. Read it. Also, to understand the idea of nuance in literature, I recommend Kosaku Takii's works, since he writes only in nuances. For you, reading these writers will benefit you more than reading Dostoevsky.

At the same time, I recommend that you take in painting and music. Never forget, writing fiction means to create a beautiful form. More strenuous matters follow, but you are not ready for these. If you have questions, please write.

Hideo

The last page was addressed to my husband Michinao.

Dear Michinao,

I promised to send you sweet cakes from the Toraya, but I have to apologize for not keeping my promise because during my wanderings in Kobe I spent all my money and couldn't even return to nearby Nara. But while I'm here, I will fulfil my promise.

Osaka has been unbearable, but recently I have come to appreciate its good aspects. As individuals, Osaka people are intolerable, but taken as a whole there is something beautiful about them.

Two or three days ago, the weather suddenly turned cold.

Are you busy as usual? I have started writing, but not to my entire satisfaction.

I ask of you somehow to look after my mother. Her nervousness must present a problem, but I ask you to care for her.

Till next time.

Hideo

Reading this letter now after so many years, I sense his tenderness toward me much more than I had noticed it then. For a person so slow to understand like me only now can I appreciate his painstaking care in attempting to explain things.

The year after father died and mother was convalescing during autumn in Kamakura, Hideo was hospitalized with appendicitis. Because the operation had been delayed, it developed into peritonitis and the situation became critical. Neither Hideo nor I knew of this condition. Confined to bed and unable to move, he passed his time reading, always jotting titles of two or three books on a piece of paper, which he asked me to buy and bring on my next visit.

One day after mid-November, I had just arrived at the hospital when Aunt Wakana Jōya, who rarely travelled to Tokyo, appeared. I was a bit surprised to see her, but she soon left and did not appear anxious. Only later did I learn that the doctor had notified our uncles of Hideo's critical condition, but had instructed them not to inform mother. It was Aunt Wakana who had rushed to the hospital. However, Hideo recovered marvellously and came home to recuperate. We had a nurse come and live with us for a while. She was a kind nurse who patiently and carefully cared for Hideo. I remember Hideo speaking to her ever so politely, "Please, if you will, do this for me. Sorry to trouble you so much...."

In time he recovered, and from the next year, he commuted to the First Higher School and began his writing activities, completing his first novel that year. I took pride in seeing Hideo attend Japan's most elite institution, the First Higher School.

In those days, First Higher School students wore their uniforms roughly by crumpling and folding their white-striped caps, hanging dirty towels from their belts, and walking about in tall wooden clogs. They intentionally adopted an air of toughness, which awed the girl students. For the Memorial Festival, girls made a big fuss about going to the First Higher School to see its attractions. I too went and invited three girl friends. I thought Hideo owed them a simple sweet-bean soup treat since they had kindly purchased tickets to his mandolin concert.

Among the crowd of students walking about, I finally spotted Hideo and introduced my three girl friends to him. Then I said, "Treat us to something."

In his dirty school-uniform trousers, Hideo walked ahead of us, clip-clopping on his tall wooden clogs. Bypassing the student shop offering sweet-bean soup, he led us into the temporary shop set up by Aokidō (a noted chain of cake-snack shops then) and seated us at a table. He ordered Western tea and cake for us; his extravagance startled me, since this treat cost far more than sweet-bean soup.

"I have to go *sake*-drinking with friends, so excuse me," he said, then took off his tattered cap, sharply bowed, and left the shop. I ate my cake, a rare treat, worrying that the cake must have depleted his small allowance.

That fall, Hideo's maiden publication, "Tako no Jisatsu" (The Suicide of the Octopus), appeared in the coterie magazine *Kyōon*, but I was unaware that the writer Naoya Shiga had praised the work. Although without really understanding it, I had concluded that it was a poor work of fiction, I immediately recognized that he had taken our friend Yoshiko as the model for the girl Yaeko in the novella. Yoshiko had said the same words as the heroine of the novella. We had met Yoshiko, the daughter of a wealthy acquaintance of Uncle Moku Jōya in Kamakura, at his house in the summer, and later swam with her at the beach.

When I was in middle school, people went to the beach to learn swimming, since few schools had pools for swimming classes. Hideo, however, was a good swimmer, having gone swimming at Tadoku Island in Mie prefecture since he was in first and second grades, his tan turning almost black, and in the upper grades he had gone with Mr Ozawa to swim at Chiba prefecture. Yoshiko was unable to swim though she lived in Kamakura, so she always came with a rubber tube to the beach. Hideo taught us to swim by first having us float with our faces in the water. Deciding to start swimming around three o'clock to avoid the mid-afternoon sun, we often met her at the beach then. After teaching us to swim in the shallow water, he used to swim alone far out until his sunburnt head would nearly disappear into the waves. Thanks to Hideo I can swim a little even today. Yoshiko too had apparently learned to breast stroke.

I then sensed by Hideo's manners that he had taken a liking to Yoshiko. She was two or three years older than me and a pretty girl who, in comparison to my crude speech, spoke politely. I met Yoshiko only at Uncle Moku's house or at the beach, but Hideo had once been invited to her house. Later he visited her two or three times.

After his first visit I asked Hideo some childish questions: "Did you have fun? How was it?"

He answered vaguely, "Well... it's an enormous house, Yoshiko's," cutting his reply short after describing the house. I couldn't help feeling that Yoshiko had become Hideo's first love.

Then I wanted to read the book, *Ai to Ninshiki to no Shuppatsu* (The Beginning of Love and Cognition), which Hideo mentioned in his first novel. I had read the play *Shukke to Sono Deshi* (The Priest and His Disciples) by the same author, Hyakuzō Kurata, and found it interesting. But I knew nothing about his essay, which seemed too advanced for me, but was then popular among young people.

I asked a Girls' Middle School classmate to check out *The Beginning of Love and Cognition* when she went to the library. She later explained that she had to repeat the difficult title to herself along the way to remember it. However, I have no recollection of whether she had ever borrowed the book or whether I ever read it.

Chapter 8
Why Can't We Live Together?

After the Great Kantō Earthquake in 1923, we worried most about mother who was convalescing in Kamakura. Telegraph and telephone lines were down. We were informed only by extra newspaper editions or rumours, making it difficult to know what was actually happening. Rumour had it that the Shōnan area, which included Kamakura, had been totally inundated by a tidal wave.

Since all transportation had come to a halt, Hideo had decided to walk to Kamakura to check on our mother. He went to Tetsutarō Kawakami's home nearby to borrow a knapsack, but finding him out he asked his mother, "I'd like to borrow a knapsack. I want to find my mother and take her some provisions."

She willingly lent Hideo a knapsack, and later remarked to Tetsutarō Kawakami how moving it was to see Hideo so worried about his mother. Hearing then that the navy was sending a ship to Kamakura on 6 September, he boarded it and arrived at Kamakura with the knapsack packed with food, clothing and daily necessities.

He found both mother's and Uncle Moku's houses had collapsed in the quake, but everyone had escaped injury. Hearing over the radio of the impending tidal wave, they had taken refuge on a mountain behind the houses. After the threat of the tidal wave ebbed, they had put together a temporary shelter in Uncle Moku's yard. This is where Hideo found mother living with the Moku Jōyas.

Hideo stayed about a week in Kamakura, cleaning out and putting in order the inside of the collapsed house. A photograph shows mother, the maid and some others in front of the house together with Hideo standing heroically with a sweatband tied around his head.

Early the following year, mother's health improved considerably, and she returned to Tokyo. We finally sold the Shirokane house and rented a small house in Mabashi in Kōenji. Though we had sold the house—as mentioned before—my mother, Hideo and I moved in with low spirits because we did not receive most of the money owed to us. Nevertheless, we felt the joy of living together with mother once again after more than two years apart.

We also took joy in the trip to the Kansai area. A month or so later, around the end of March, after we had moved to Kōenji, my father's eldest brother, Uncle Seiichirō Shimizu, who lived in Kyoto, visited Tokyo, timing his trip to coincide with the memorial visit to our father's grave. Previously, he had stayed at the Shirokane house during his Tokyo trips, but this time he stayed in an inn in Ueno, thinking our Mabashi house too small. As he prepared to return home, he invited Hideo and me to Kyoto and Nara for a sightseeing trip. I had never been there before as father's death and other preoccupations had prevented me from joining my upper-grade class at the girls' middle school on several excursions to the Kansai area. It was near the end of spring vacation, and the trip meant we would have to be absent from school but still mother consented and we hastily packed. Of course, Uncle Shimizu was to pay for the entire trip.

Mother stayed up all night and sewed a *haori* coat made of *omeshi* cloth for me to use on the trip, my first one since father's death. I left for Kansai wearing that *haori* with my single, sole *yūzenchirimen* kimono, my maroon *hakama* skirt and lace-up shoes.

Uncle Seiichiro ran a large bookstore that sold sutras and Buddhist books in central Kyoto in front of Nishihonganji Temple. His small, elongated dwelling with quadrangular flagstones was located behind the store. Most interesting for me were the small, traditional household items kept in a compact room in this Kyoto-style house.

We took in all the noteworthy spots in Kyoto, including Maruyama Park where cherry trees stood. We also saw a full troupe of geisha and young dancing-girls perform the Miyako Dance magnificently in Gion district. Uncle Jūemon Nishimura, who lived in Yamashina in Kyoto, took us to see them. Also, Hideo went alone to visit the writer Naoya Shiga at his home in Yamashina.

We also visited Nara. At the Hōryūji Temple, Hideo looked at the Yumedono Kannon statue for so long that my cousin, who took us, and I tired of waiting. Later, I realized that Naoya Shiga had advised Hideo to study that statue well. We went to Chūgūji Temple, the first time for all of us, including our Kyoto-reared cousin. Now it became Hideo's turn to serve as a guide, explaining the splendour of the Mirokubosatsu statue in the main sanctuary; it was a wooden-statue called Hankashiizō, a wonderful example of Asuka Period sculpture—a smiling Buddha with the right hand lifted to the cheek.

A nun led us to the statue, and Hideo brashly pressed his face to it. The Kannon's face was so splendid I could not pull myself away either. Then Hideo walked around to the rear and studied it intently. Our cousin, impatient at having to stay so long, sat waiting in front of the statue. I too grew anxious as the nun stared, frowning at my brother.

We took in other old Buddhist statues and the unusual and beautiful spring scenery of Kyoto, then returned to Tokyo happy and contented. Hideo, too, in his way, had fully enjoyed the sights. This occasion, however, turned out to be the last trip that Hideo and I were to take together.

That year, Hideo joined others in forming a coterie magazine, *Seidō Jidai* (Bronze Age), to which he submitted various pieces, then he started another coterie magazine, *Yama Mayu* (Cocoon Mountain), with Tatsuo Nagai and others. His writing was in full swing again.

Mother, though never too healthy, took in sewing from her neighbours and went to teach flower arrangement and the tea ceremony, which she was encouraging me to learn. I, however, was preoccupied with my college studies, a part-time job and writing a novel, so I didn't comply. At the time, department stores would exhibit her flower arrangements, but never once did Hideo and I go to see them. Mother once said resentfully that her acquaintances' sons and daughters were encouraging each other to go. Only after mother died in 1946 did I begin to feel how irresponsible I had been as a daughter and to blame myself for not attending even once.

Hideo's lack of responsibility, however, was far worse, I thought. At nights, if he was home, he merely spent the time drinking and loudly debating with three or four young writer friends.

In this group, a small, pale-faced young man with his hair cut "bowl style" to his eyebrows joined the literary coterie. This lad was a heavy drinker who usually drank until he was totally inebriated. Spotting our tortoise-shell cat, he would yell out, "Hey, philosopher!" and try to catch it, but never succeeded. When he wasn't drunk, he changed into an extremely quiet lad, who greeted me in ever so gentlemanly a way. He was the poet, Chūya Nakahara, then aged seventeen or eighteen.

Two or three times, he brought a beautiful girl who appeared much older than he, and much taller. She had her bowl-style black hair cut at her forehead like Nakahara's, and her face seemed overly large. Her big eyes and dashing features made her appear non-Japanese. Hideo later explained that she was Nakahara's girlfriend, an understudy actress at Makino Productions.

I was occupied with my college studies and other matters. I left home early every morning and didn't return until evening, often not seeing Hideo for a whole week. Even when he was at home, he rarely had time to talk with us, burying his head in writing or studying at his desk. We seldom had supper together as a family to talk in a leisurely way about our day's activities, our future, or our favourite food. Whenever my mother and I happened to be together, we usually complained to each other about Hideo.

Hideo entered Tokyo Imperial University in April 1925, but early that month took a trip to Ogasawara Island with an acquaintance, Shuttō, supposedly a university student boarding nearby in Mabashi. I was thrown into a rage, thinking that Hideo had egocentrically spent money on the trip at a time when our frail mother was taking in sewing to make ends meet. However, I learned later that his acquaintance, Shuttō, had paid for most of the trip. Hideo had met him just before the trip at the landlord's tennis court nearby. Shuttō always wore a square school cap and university uniform. He was sociable, often striking up a conversation with mother. He seemed to have money, lavishing it on the Ogasawara trip and once treating my mother and me to a kabuki play. One day, however, when he and I were alone, he suddenly tried to kiss me. After that I never laid eyes on him again. Apparently soon after that he left the area.

Later, neighbourhood rumour held that Shuttō was an imposter, a well-known braggart and not enrolled in any university.

In early October that year, Hideo took another trip, this time to Ōshima Island. I was again angered, thinking him selfish. But I knew nothing about what had transpired between Hideo and his drinking friends, particularly between Hideo and Chūya Nakahara. That April Hideo had first met Chūya's girlfriend Yasuko and by July she had become his girlfriend. Nor did I know about Hideo's despair.

When he returned from Ōshima Island, he began to suffer from severe abdominal pains. He was diagnosed as having twisted intestines, was hospitalized and required an operation. Unable to pay the hospital bills, with the doctor's help, we placed him in a charity hospital in Izumibashi. He lay in bed at one corner of a large, plain room lined with beds full of patients. On my second visit after his operation, I was surprised to see Nakahara's girlfriend sitting on his bed.

I wondered about Hideo's relationship with Yasuko, but without further ado I simply greeted her, finished my visit, and left. She had sat motionless throughout.

It was after Hideo had been discharged, and in the later half of November, that Hideo came to my three-mat room near the front entrance with a serious look and said, "I want you to understand something."

Tense, I sat up and faced him. He dropped himself to a sitting position, and unloaded the bombshell. He had decided to move out and live with that girl. I could not believe it! Realizing for the first time how deeply involved he was with Yasuko, I did not inquire further about Chūya Nakahara. His planning to leave mother and me was a far more serious matter.

"Why can't we all live together? Mother and I can get to like her if it's someone you like."

"It's difficult to actually live together with her. It won't work out. Anyhow, say you agree."

I thought it useless to say any more. I felt angry tears welling in my eyes. They expressed both a bitterness toward Hideo for his already having brought us suffering and now abandoning us for that girl, and a deep pity for my saddened, forsaken mother. On the other hand, studying in my senior year in college and concerned about my own affairs, I could not care less about him, though I could not completely rid myself of the anger I felt for his abandoning us.

To begin his new household, he sold everything—the last large bookcase we had, the complete works of the Japanese classics in it, and the few remaining ceramics my father had liked, and even his old tools.

In his now vacant eight-mat room, Hideo spread a huge cloth into which he folded his quilts and placed his other belongings. My face puffing with anger, I helped by shoving in his books and some breakables between the folded quilt.

The slow movements of mother's thin back expressed an air of abandoned loneliness as she quietly removed his clothing and underclothes from the drawers and folded them in the cloth.

Hideo's new dwelling was a small three-room rented cottage, located near the tracks on the opposite side of Kōenji Station from us.

Chapter 9
To Complain Daily Is A Waste Of Time

Until Hideo told me about living with Nakahara's lover, I had known nothing about Hideo's relationship with her. His words came like a bolt from the blue. I was that insensitive and such a latecomer regarding romance, so childish and immature.

This reminds me of something that happened some six years before, in 1919. It was two years before Hideo entered First Higher School, and I was in my third year of Tokyo Prefectural Third Girls' Middle School.* We were still living at Shirokane.

We had then a family doctor, Dr Kimura, who had cared for mother and later treated Hideo's appendicitis in 1921. Dr Kimura's son, Osamu, was Hideo's classmate at First Middle School. He did not take an interest in literature but played mandolin with Hideo and often used to come to our house, so I knew him too. Both failed the entrance exam to First Higher School, then spent the following year together in private study. They were close friends: they had also become lost on a mountain climbing trip where they barely escaped death; and they rented a cottage on the Chiba coastline where they lived, cooking and studying together in the summer of 1920. The following year, in March 1921, both passed the First Higher School exams and soon formed the Crescent Mandolin Club together.

That day in 1919, Hideo instructed me, "Osamu Kimura wants to talk with you, so wait at Meguro Station on your way back from school."

In contrast to teenagers today, I was terribly childish for a girl of fifteen, cutely dressed in a cotton kimono with shoulder tucks, and a maroon *hakama* skirt. I was not particularly interested in boys but, rather, keen on the serious talk. I rode the trolley past the usual Hiyoshizakaue stop to Meguro Station, the end of the line.

Hideo and Osamu were waiting; Hideo immediately scurried off as I approached.

---

* Then located in Roppongi but now in Komaba.

Osamu, then about seventeen, walked out of the station, I quietly followed him. After walking along the street on which trolley tracks ran, we saw a cemetery into which we turned. I remember seeing a temple inside the cemetery, but Osamu headed towards an isolated area. I felt a little jittery but, thinking him to be harmless, I tagged along. Somewhere in the central part of the cemetery, Osamu stopped and turned to face me, looking disturbed.

We looked quietly at each other, then Osamu squatted, so I squatted too. Osamu fidgeted and faltered. I looked into his face, then shifted my gaze to the grave nearby and waited. After a while, I boldly asked, "What is it? Tell me what you want!"

Osamu placed his hands on his head, then brushed his hand against his forehead, looking up and down.

Finally he said, "Oh nothing. Nothing at all." Then he stood up.

All tension in me gave way and I stood up exasperated. When I started to walk back, he led me to the trolley street, where he turned around and made a salute with his cap, saying, "See you later." Then he quickly disappeared.

I returned home despondent, wondering what Osamu had wanted to say. Hideo had not yet returned home, coming back only before suppertime. He remained silent, so that night I finally confronted him.

"Why did Osamu ask me to that isolated place? He hardly said anything."

Hideo quietly picked up his mandolin and began to strum it. He didn't say a word, though I waited for some time.

Many years later I realized I must have stunned Osamu into silence, a simpleton like me unable to sense a boy's love for a girl. He had probably prepared a line, but couldn't speak them to so childish a girl as me. If it was any other matter, Hideo would probably have explained things, but on this occasion he remained silent, concluding I would not understand.

I was so naive that when I saw Yasuko seated near Hideo's bed at Izumibashi Hospital that November, I was startled but suspected nothing.

Only recently, after Hideo's death, did I read articles about the events leading to their living together.

Only the gods know, however, what actually happened. Since even eyewitnesses often fail to give accurate testimony, to explain or write about events is much more difficult.

After Hideo's death, well-known literati and most of his friends wrote memoirs about him. Many accounts were far from the truth, even by those more intimate with Hideo than me, his friends who had travelled and gone golfing with him. Perhaps, by nature, people are prone to be irresponsible in an unconscious way.

In May 1983, an exclusive interview with Yasuko, Nakahara's lover and later Hideo's partner, was re-published. There is also a synopsis of an account by Yasuko, which had originally been published in 1974.

No doubt she knows best about what had occurred between them. So, reading her interview, I understood their relationship at last. She mentions not only Hideo, but also Chūya Nakahara, myself, my mother and the Kobayashi family, as well as what occurred after Hideo had left her. However, she makes many errors. So much so that her account in "Kobayashi Hideo no Omoide" (Reminiscences of Hideo Kobayashi) frankly leads me to believe that she has turned senile. Also, her 1974 account includes so many mistakes that I believe they originated in her, not only from her fear of contamination.

Nonetheless, Yasuko's unusual, eccentric ways probably attracted both Chūya Nakahara and Hideo as young men. Perhaps she was attractive from a man's standpoint, but from my perspective as a woman, she was not in the least sexy and lacked the soft, gentle touch. She stood tall and bony and though she was pretty she spoke rudely like a man and wore strange clothes which were out of place and distracting. Occasionally she spoke with some intelligence, but seemingly without understanding her own words, which made intimate conversation with her difficult.

Calling me "Fuji-chan, Fuji-chan", she was friendly enough and good-natured, but remained too complex a person for me to fathom.

After Hideo left her, he wrote from Kansai "That girl lacks heart, so thoroughly that...", a fact which took him three years to realize.

Next, in the 1983 interview, Yasuko mentions Hideo's death.

> It happened so long ago. I merely thought... so he has passed away. But that man did lead me to the new religion called Kyūseikyō. He was a devotee of Kyūseikyō.

She talks of Hideo so casually that I was more dumbfounded than angry. No matter how long ago, he had once loved and cared for her when she was ill, even at the risk of endangering his own life. Even adult men wept before Hideo's corpse and his photograph during his funeral. Also, how far-fetched is her account that Hideo had led her to the Kyūseikyō religion. It was not until 1939 or 1940 that my mother had become a member and insisted that Hideo also join, which he did briefly for her sake.

Around 1925, when Chūya Nakahara and Yasuko lived in Kōenji and often visited our Mabashi house, all was not going well between them, with her fear of contamination acting up.

In July, when Nakahara had returned to his hometown, Hideo paid Yasuko a visit. Yasuko tells how Hideo, drenched from an evening shower, had asked for a rag to wipe his muddy feet before entering, and that, as she served him tea, Hideo had kissed her on her cheek. This apparently was the beginning of their relationship behind Nakahara's back. Nakahara had been neglecting her, leaving her alone at home. When Hideo happened to visit and behaved tenderly towards her, this slowly drew her to Hideo.

Around that summer in 1925, I was unaware of Hideo's relationship with Yasuko, so absorbed was I in thinking about my own plans.

From the previous year, I had been yearning to go to Karuizawa. I was looking for a summer job there—a place of refuge from the hot summer, where many Westerners also stayed.

I was finally offered an ideal job there as a live-in tutor: I taught two teen-age daughters of a wealthy family at their Karuizawa villa. Their parents were too busy to come; they had also rented another villa in Karuizawa for three other sons to live with a student as a tutor and overseer.

I left Tokyo that summer with thoughts of taking walks in the fresh mountain air, studying and reading my favourite books in my spare time in the coolness of Karuizawa.

In the 1920s, Karuizawa was not as crowded in summer as today. The streets were quiet, and filled with many Westerners. I found most interesting the Western ladies walking with Japanese *haori* coats slipped over their Western dresses.

So the first week, everything was fun, with new places to take in and see. After finishing a morning session of studies, the girls and I enjoyed the day going for walks on the empty roads among the larch-tree forests, climbing Mount Atago, going to high scenic spots and walking towards Mount Hanare, then planning for self-study hours.

However, the days grew routine. I found little time for myself. From morning to night I had to live with and oversee the girls who were already fifteen and thirteen years old. Since I had a separate room, I got them to do their own reading and studying so I could study in my room, but not ten minutes would pass before they had questions, or began to bicker and quarrel. When I went in to calm them, they would suggest that we visit their brothers' villa or walk through the town at night.

Also, their brothers would want to return the visit, wanting to light fireworks or to play cards. Also, they invited us to see Western children perform the play *Robin Hood*, or the famous actress Yaeko Mizutani perform a Japanese dance. Though not interested in going, I had to chaperone the girls. This was fine for those without studies who came to escape the summer heat or to enjoy their summer; but I only grew increasingly frustrated, unable to do any reading, thinking or writing. Fully irritated, I complained by letter to Hideo in Tokyo about my deep dissatisfaction. I was mistaken in thinking that I could study and read in the Karuizawa coolness; I could not find any free time for thought, I was looking after the girls every day, and did not enjoy this at all.

Knowing how lax Hideo was, I did not expect a quick reply, but a postcard arrived within a few days.

[postmarked August 1925 but undated]

Fujiko,

To complain every day is time wasted. Treasure each moment of the present. You supposedly went there in order to teach, but teaching is impossible without love. Complaining that you lack time for your reading is selfish. Take better care of the girls, enjoy their activities with them, and go and have a love affair.

Hideo

From Hideo's short note, I realized how wrong I had been. In college I had repeatedly learned that "education is love". I understood then, but I had failed to apply this lesson. Selfishly, I had presumed myself an effective teacher by studying hard and dutifully teaching all that I knew, but I had failed miserably in loving the girls.

I fully appreciated the sincerity of Hideo's reply when I later learned how painful his relationship was with Yasuko then. I learned five vital truths: (1) to spend each day complaining is time wasted; (2) to value the present and to live fully is most important; (3) to truly teach, I must love and care for the girls, as I had learnt at college; (4) to think selfishly and to neglect others is wrong; (5) to enjoy activities with the girls means to become one with them, unless you do this, i.e. enjoy what they do, you can't understand what they feel.

Perhaps the two teenagers had not noticed, but I changed as a teacher after receiving Hideo's postcard. I thereafter found each day more enjoyable and profitable.

His last piece of advice, however, to "go and have a love affair", I failed miserably to heed. I met only the tutor of the girls' three brothers, and the big brother of a friend of the two girls, who was in Karuizawa for the summer. The tutor was an honest, serious-minded student, but not the type to make me fall in love. The villa of the girls' friend had a tennis court, so when I was invited there, I went to play tennis with the big brother of the girls' friend. But since I had only ever played tennis with a big rubber ball and not regular tennis, I hit most of the balls out of court and returned home in shame.

Only later did I understand why Hideo had written "go and have a love affair". Though Hideo's love was perhaps illicit and caused him much suffering, he nevertheless accepted it in all sincerity. He had realized that loving another person—particularly of the opposite sex—enriched, matured and brought joy to him. All this he desired also for his sister. I didn't understand this then, not until much later did I sense his consideration for me in his simple words. This only deepens my grief for Hideo.

About that time, Hideo had told Yasuko, "Your thoughts are like Nakahara's but your feelings are like mine."

By summer he had fallen deeply in love with her, but he was blind to her character, I believe. Still young, Hideo had idealized her, as in the adages "Even a pockmark appears a dimple" and "Love is without reason", which Hideo understood later, when he realized that Yasuko did not suit him, either intellectually or emotionally.

Hideo possessed a pure, blind love for her. He undoubtedly sought with all his power to help to cure her, to reinstate a sense of humanity and character in her. To accomplish this, he had endured and had been patient, but he was exhausted.

Having advised me to "go and have a love affair", Hideo was to suffer a mortal agony, and at seeing all his efforts end in failure he had no choice but to immorally abandon her. However, I believe Hideo did the right thing, since he had no other recourse open to him. This tragedy had served to deepen and broaden Hideo's character and mould him into the man he was later to become.

Thanks to Hideo's advice, I enjoyed the summer and a rich experience. I returned to Tokyo safely with the two girls.

In September, their parents invited me with the girls to the Imperial Hotel for supper. Their gratitude far exceeded my expectations.

Chapter 10
It's Unbearable, So Don't Come

In October 1925, Hideo took a trip to Ōshima Island. I was bitterly angry about this, not knowing his situation and thinking he was again squandering money we direly needed.

Hideo was planning to take Yasuko to Ōshima Island, but when he suggested, "Let's go to Ōshima", she did not reply favourably. She was worried not about Nakahara but about her future as an actress in the New Drama Theatre. Nonetheless, sensing a romantic trip with Hideo, she later agreed to go with him.

That day Nakahara left home in the morning, and Yasuko began preparations for this secret trip. She had arranged to meet Hideo at Shinagawa Station at one o'clock, but a rain shower forced her to return home. Anxious to leave but unable to, she finally brought herself to say to Nakahara, "I'm stepping out a moment." She arrived at two o'clock at Shinagawa Station, but Hideo had already departed for Ōshima Island alone.

Whether he was planning to do so beforehand or felt betrayed by Yasuko, once at Ōshima Island, he thought of suicide. Hideo had not said a word to me about this. I knew nothing of his brooding state, which I later felt apologetic about. How sorry I felt for him then, I understood only a few years later.

However, the gods—whose awesomeness Hideo sensed on the island—had not forsaken him. On the verge of contemplating death, something solemn impressed upon him that life was not his to waste by suicide. He had grasped hold of a transcendent god, a power beyond humankind.

Unable to take his own life, Hideo returned to Tokyo. Just to imagine his mental state upon his return, I find unbearable. Perhaps as a result of his agony, he suffered abdominal pains caused by twisted intestines and had to be hospitalized, and then operated upon. It was in that October that I was surprised to see Yasuko at the hospital.

According to Yasuko's account, while Hideo was convalescing, he had said in the hallway, "Let's live together." We cannot know what they spoke about at the hospital beforehand, but they had made their decision. It was upon his discharge that Hideo left our Mabashi house to live with Yasuko in a rented house in nearby Amanuma, Kōenji.

As for Nakahara, he apparently frequented their house while Hideo was away at university, quarrelling and fighting, even hitting and knocking Yasuko down.

I knew nothing of this, since I only dropped in to bring some belongings and books requested by Hideo on my way back from college. She always sat formally in one spot on a knee blanket spread on a straw mat. She sat motionless. Our talk was routine, but I was shocked at the disarray of the house. At the entrance, rice bowls, just eaten out of, were stacked high. The room had books, magazines, written manuscripts, scraps of paper and newspapers scattered about, leaving almost nowhere to walk. The alcove served as a closet, with shirts, clothing and odds-and-ends piled up high. The wooden floor of the alcove, where it was visible, had layers of dust that could be seen even from a distance.

But Hideo always spoke optimistically, saying, "We couldn't forever eat only buckwheat noodles, and we soon tired of egg, or chicken on rice. So nowadays we have hot rice delivered in bowls, on which we pile fermented beans. It's nutritious and so-o-o tasty."

Hideo always talked to me cheerfully. Yasuko in her illness could do nothing, so I admired Hideo for putting up with this sort of life. Never did he show a gloomy face or complain to mother or me. Mother, however, learned of their situation and prepared meals for them occasionally, which she had me deliver.

For a livelihood, Hideo translated and tutored, but Yasuko's illness hampered his work, so he decided to try living with us. He thought the change might help her illness since she could have three nourishing meals a day, not to mention the financial benefits of living together. Mother, too, was worried about Yasuko. A name-omen reader had told mother that changing Yasuko's ill-omened name would cure her. Mother renamed her Sakiko, after which we all called her Sakiko.

She very seldom came out of her four-and-a-half-mat room. Whether Sakiko went out alone or with Hideo, whenever she returned home she would have long arguments with him in the room.

Hideo was always concerned about her illness. He complied with her every whim, doing whatever he could to cure her. They lived with us under such trying circumstances for less than two months. They moved again, this time to Hase, Kamakura. He thought that perhaps the ocean and the favourable climate might improve her condition. Intending to visit them, I received detailed directions to their house, but before I could visit they had moved to the adjoining town, Zushi. Hideo had lived with Sakiko exactly a year after first leaving the Mabashi house.

I had graduated from college, and in the following April became a teacher in a girls' middle school in Kitasenju, Tokyo. The Mabashi house was too far, so I moved with my mother to Tennōji near Nippori Station into an old rented house in front of Yanaka Cemetery.

In the meantime, Hideo and Sakiko had moved back to Tokyo, to Shirokane-dai, near Uncle Saburō's house. Uncle Saburō and Aunt Yūko greatly assisted during their time there. Uncle Saburō, who had grown up with us from his middle school days to his young adulthood, regarded Hideo as a younger brother. Apparently, Hideo had no hesitation in making requests, and received more than favourable treatment.

Sakiko's illness grew worse, so Hideo called me and said: "Don't come to our home. When she's with others, she is in good spirits, but afterwards she falls into terrible spells. These fits are absolutely unbearable, so don't come." Thus, though I occasionally dropped in at Uncle Saburō's, I never visited Hideo.

In the 1920s, trolleys ran along Shirokane-dai Street. I later learned that, during a walk on this street, Sakiko had begun quarrelling with Hideo and pushed Hideo towards an oncoming trolley in an hysterical rage. Hideo was nearly run over and killed. Sakiko apparently had threatened to take Hideo's life on many occasions.

Four months after they moved to Shirokane-dai, they moved to Yato in Higashi Nakano in February 1928. It was about fifteen minutes' walk from the south exit of Higashi Nakano Station in one of the seven to eight small houses on the lot, with some tennis courts on the west side. In one of the houses the landlord, Tai Matsumoto, and his wife lived.

The landlord's wife, Keiko, a graduate of the English Literature Department of Aoyama Gakuin University, had studied in England, where she met and married Tai Matsumoto. Returning to Japan, she published many translations of children's books. Good to others, she asked me to assist her on a part-time basis in rewriting manuscripts and other jobs, while I taught at middle school. In front of the Matsumotos lived a young man named Takamizawa, an art school graduate and a member of MAVO, a group headed by the avant-garde artist Tomoyoshi Maruyama. Takamizawa was painting with unreserved freedom, hanging empty cans and human hair on canvas. He wore his long hair parted in the centre and hanging down to his shoulders, dressed in an old *rubashka*,* and had painted the whole exterior of his house with abstract pictures of numerous colours. He occasionally visited the Matsumotos, where I met him, but I had dismissed him as an eccentric.

To my great surprise, Hideo and Sakiko moved to the rented house behind Takamizawa's. I hadn't seen Hideo for almost a year. He looked totally

---

* Russian men's clothing worn at home.

exhausted. But Sakiko, on the other hand, appeared healthy before others and struck up a friendship with Mrs Matsumoto.

Hideo met Takamizawa, and evidently said to Sakiko, "That fellow's a little affected," but had come to detect some humanity in him.

Though Hideo's move to Yato caught me as a pleasant surprise, I rarely visited Hideo's, unless when absolutely necessary. Hideo had instructed me not to visit them, and Hideo's face showed that Sakiko's illness had become worse.

It occurred some three months after they had moved to Yato. If her account is correct, Sakiko had visited the place of a male friend in nearby Nakano, and was escorted by him to her home late that night of 25 May.

The fellow left, but Sakiko had gone into a tantrum when Hideo did not thank her escort properly and failed to reply adequately to her nonsensical questions. Then she yelled, "Get out!"

It was about 2 a.m. when Hideo left, with only the casual kimono and wooden clogs he wore. He never returned. Apparently, previously she had yelled, "Get out!" in uncontrollable fits, but he had never walked out on her.

Hideo had failed to return after two or three days, but Sakiko remained confident he would return. After a week, however, I started to worry. Keiko Matsumoto blamed Hideo. Sympathizing with the abandoned Sakiko, she fed Sakiko three times a day at her home and looked after her. It was then that I received Hideo's first Kansai letter, as already mentioned.

At long last, with this letter, I understood Hideo for the first time. The Hideo who had been so distant from me had drawn closer to me; tears came to my eyes as I read the letter many times over. I deeply apologized to him. Although sympathizing with his sufferings, until then I had loathed him, thinking he had ignored my mother and me.

I also wanted to inform Keiko Matsumoto about Hideo's feelings, but the letter instructed me, "Don't say anything about my running away," and so I said nothing about Hideo's whereabouts.

Keiko severely blamed Hideo. "How cruel of him. Regardless of his feelings changing towards her or his no longer loving her, to abandon his former love to the streets is going too far. No longer liking her, he needs to settle with her and to provide for her livelihood. When you learn of his whereabouts, please make this point clear. What's wrong with him anyway? Sakiko is in a pitiful state too, you know."

Since Keiko knew nothing of Sakiko's illness, her position was understandable.

I too felt that Hideo would come back, seeing Sakiko so confident of Hideo's return and knowing that Hideo had previously loved her so.

Perhaps in my third letter to Hideo, I wrote that Keiko was caring for Sakiko and assuring others that he would return, but I wanted to know his true feelings towards her. He responded by filling seven manuscript pages, each with 220 spaces for characters—printed on the upper right-hand corner were the words "Buddha's spirit manuscript paper".

Chapter 11
Happiness Is So Terribly Commonplace

Hideo abandoned Sakiko, and took refuge in a Nichiren Temple in Osaka. Why he went to this particular temple is not clear, but apparently a friend had found it for him or had been renting a room there.

Prior to his lengthy letter that had described his agony with Sakiko, I had already received three.

His letter in answer to my reply to his first letter was brief.

> Dear Fujiko,
>
> Thanks for your letter.
>
> Everyday I find something irritating. This temple is too big for me. I plan to move to another lodging soon.
>
> Now, I am at a loss how to rewrite the article for *Kaizō* magazine.
>
> Please write to me about anything. You don't have to worry.
>
> Osaka is an unpleasant place. Only the trains are convenient.
>
> I want to go to Uncle's place, but I have only the kimono I am wearing.
>
> Give my regards to mother.
>
> Hideo

Uncle refers to Uncle Seiichirō Shimizu, who had invited us to go sightseeing in Kyoto and Nara in 1924.

I immediately sent Hideo some kimonos as requested, then wrote him a letter about my own affairs—about the possibility of my marriage, a writer who said he liked me, and other matters. Hideo was the only one I could consult with about such personal matters.

I received his third Kansai letter written with a brush on blue-lined Japanese stationery.

> Dear Fujiko,
>
> I have read your letter. Thanks for the kimonos that you sent the other day. I intended to stay at the temple but the temple has serious

problems about which I am forced to listen and feel sorry. Also a fellow called Sano is coming to Kyoto, so I went to Uncle Shimizu in Kyoto to explain the entire situation, and asked his help, to which he consented. I plan to stay around here, free of worries. Uncle has kindly understood mother's position, and that my trouble with Yasuko might inconvenience him. About this, please have mother write to Uncle Shimizu. Keichan's marriage to the girl didn't fare well, and they separated last year. I also met Uncle Nishimura yesterday. He now lives in Suita, a suburb of Osaka....

About someone proposing to you, I don't know the fellow so I can't say anything. First of all, such a matter is an individual's secret, which a third person cannot possibly fathom. But anyway, I suggest that you write as much about him as possible to me.

I can't comment on this fellow Nakamura, without seeing his writing. However, a person who intends "aesthetic" writing and truly has this capacity is rarer than a pearl at the ocean bottom. This is a fact.

Much effort is required before one is able to see the true goodness or badness in a fellow. When looking at a person, don't look into his intellectual thoughts. These are only conceived ideas, not his humanity. Man's goodness or badness is not seen in conceived ideas. In general, as Aristotle said, man's goals in life do not reside in his concepts apart from his lifestyle, which determines his happiness and misfortunes. Man only needs to find a worthy lifestyle. A person doubting this is headed for hell, since otherwise the entrance into hell is reserved only for geniuses. Tolstoy says man's misfortunes differ with each individual, but man's happinesses are all similar. How true. Simply put, it means the following. Man himself invites misfortune by resisting nature's way. It is only for this reason. Because each individual resists in varying ways, so the misfortunes appear in varying shades. Man finds happiness by becoming one with nature. To live a natural life requires a person to become one with nature, no matter who the person is. Nature has nothing dramatic. It is terribly commonplace. And so, happiness is always terribly commonplace. I suggest you read Shinran's *Tannishō* (Lamentations over Divergences). It's a book of treasures. It reveals nature's secrets.

I am in need of some Western clothes; it's so inconvenient otherwise. Since the house in Nakano is not often occupied, please ask Takamizawa to get for me my shoes and white shirts when no one is at home from the room at the far left.

My regards to mother.

Hideo

Keichan is our cousin, the only son of Uncle Shimizu, who took us around Kyoto and Nara in 1924.

Then another letter came approximately a day later, hastily scrawled and a near duplicate of the above. It began—

> Forgetting to post the letter in Osaka, I write the same letter in case you haven't received it, although I think someone posted it for me.

The letter ended with the following addition:

> I'm thinking of living in Nara. In Nara, I can live on thirty yen a month, since the rent is five or six yen. I saw a play with Uncle Nishimura last night. Yesterday I sent you a copy of *Tannishō*.

Then again a day later, the small, thin book *Tannishō* arrived. I sensed Hideo's affection for me in troubling himself to send a copy of the book, and immediately sent him a reply, thanking him. I also added that I intended to read the book, that I would send his Western clothes in the way he instructed, also that Keiko Matsumoto was angry at him, and that Sakiko was sure of his return. I wrote that I wanted to know his real feelings towards her. I also mentioned that Takamizawa had proposed marriage to me, and finally that I wished him to further explain the statement in his previous letter, "Happiness is so terribly commonplace."

About two days after sending my reply, I hand copied Hideo's first Kansai letter and the last paragraph of his fourth Kansai letter requesting his Western clothes, and brought them to Yato for Keiko Matsumoto and Takamizawa to read. I also explained to Keiko about Sakiko's illness, and added details of what I knew or could surmise. Keiko, at first unconvinced, slowly began to understand, and finally allowed us to remove Hideo's belongings from what was now Sakiko's house. At the time, Sakiko was out, and this enabled Takamizawa and myself to carry most items we could identify as Hideo's to the Takamizawa's house—his suit, white shirts, shoes, socks, neckties, bathrobe, French books, etc.

I left a note: "I'm taking my brother's things. Fujiko." Then, telling Takamizawa that I would come again in four or five days to pack and send the clothing, I returned to the Yanaka house.

Two or three days later I received the fifth Kansai letter.

> Fujiko,
> I have read your letter.
> So you want to know my true feelings. You don't understand, of course, because so much has occurred that is beyond commonsense. How troublesome are this world's commonsense type moralities and man's sentiments.

I left. That is, I abandoned a girl. I could not make it any more definite, but people have not taken it as final. I can't imagine why they think I am merely putting on an act for my mother and sister. I definitely do not intend to return; I am not playacting.

That girl lacks heart, thoroughly so. It's extremely hard to see this in her; only lately have I managed to penetrate into this secret of hers. I have been tormented and forced to bear her antics, which are beyond imagining. Thinking back on it, it was a nightmare. I have kept this hidden from mother and yourself. I had to, otherwise it would have upset you both. When mother inquired about her, I just answered, "She's much better," so as not to worry her.

For example, I couldn't recollect what she had said on the train. I couldn't remember what she had asked me, so she slapped my face on the street going home. She swore at me. Well and good, if this would satisfy her, but she refused to return home until I remembered. We wandered about past midnight. It would have been dreadful if, in a fit of anger, I should try to strike back at her. It took until morning to soothe her. This is but one example. I cannot possibly account to you all the endless other occurrences.

I, your brother, was always true to her. I answered each and every one of her thousands of foolish questions. Thousands of absurd, endless demands I carried out (she asking me to close the sliding door twice, to answer her a hundred times, to rewash the towel eighteen times—all of which is probably difficult for you to imagine). Is this an illness, or can it be an illness for the sake of convenience, since whenever I was out, she played tennis or took hot baths? Whatever it is, let's say she was ill, at least when she was with me. Confronting her craziness on a daily basis, seeing her waving a long razor at me or trying to choke me with a rope was in itself excruciating. Whether she was ill or normal, the actualities before me were beyond human forbearance, simply because of their deranged nature. She was not playacting on my behalf. Let's accept all this, as it is. Let's assume she is ill and cannot control herself. Nevertheless, her case is absolutely hopeless, since she is always indifferent, unaware of her true self. She actually believes her own words, "I am ill, so I cannot help but behave terribly. You are a fool for getting angry with me. I am doing my utmost to control myself. If you were more careful, you would not upset me. So you are the fool." This comes not from her mysophobia, or a morbid dread of dirt. I'd term it a sickness of indifference, one of "morality".

You said Mrs Matsumoto is caring for her. Then that girl must have something to deserve such care. That is all. I will not thank her, or ask that she stop caring for her. As for commonsense morality, I have cancelled my love-oath to her. But only god knows the truth of the matter. I ask that others not intrude.

Don't worry mother. Convince her I'm on a trip. Regardless of where I am, I can study. I can think about the most important things while even urinating, so don't worry.

It doesn't matter about the Western clothes. As for money, I'm broke, so send some. Address it to me c/o Hasegawa Inn, Onmae Dōri Kudaru, Aburakōji. Uncle Shimizu asked me to stay here, I suppose he didn't want Auntie worrying about me, since Keichan's turn of events was upsetting her.

I will explain the term commonplace next time. You are fortunate to have Takamizawa loving you so. Remember how rare it is for anyone to possess such love, a thing which one is apt to forget. Takamizawa is a good-natured man, not in the popular sense of being weak-willed, but in that he is pure-hearted.

[Hideo]

In Hideo's first Kansai letter, sent from the Nichiren Temple, which revealed for the first time both his indescribable agony and his love for mother and me—about which I didn't know until then—I felt the hitherto distant Hideo had drawn close to me.

However, the above fifth letter—which had described concretely his torment—caused my body to quiver, sending shivers down my spine.

How Hideo had persevered! How like a clown he had grieved! What inexpressible sadness he had concealed deep behind his usual bright countenance! How I marvelled at his forbearance—and was moved by it!

As I re-read his words "I was always true to her", tears came to my eyes. He had been true to her, and had lived his life in integrity and sincerity after all.

That I can vouch for him without hesitation arouses in me great happiness and gratefulness.

Hideo's love—fully tested during his younger days—had far from warped him, but rather had deeply enriched him in the years that followed.

Few have been critics in as vast a field as Hideo. This fact reaped for him positive and negative comments. Not without sarcasm, some people have fondly called Hideo: "The Divine Critic", "Founder", "Modern Socrates", "Supreme Japanese Thinker", "The Japanese Sage", "An Expert on Humanity", "Teacher of Life", "Man of Wisdom", "Priest of an Altarless Shrine", etc. Others have severely criticized him, almost insultingly: "Expert at Cutting Remarks", "Man without Emotions", "Mr Vulgar", "A Trickster of Paradoxes", "A Tactician, Reactionary, Dogmatician", etc.

Admittedly, these touch on some facets of Hideo and describe him in some respects, but they all fall short in describing Hideo's essence as a person. Hideo was much deeper and more incomprehensible, since he revealed only a portion of himself, the greater part remaining deep in his soul.

Among what surfaced most predominantly was Hideo's stubbornness, terrible in his younger days, which, I believe, came from his absolute honesty, refusing adamantly to compromise himself on what he felt to be true.

His first year at university, while living with Sakiko, he told the French literature professor Yutaka Tatsuno, his mentor and benefactor, "I have left home to live with a girl. I need to make a living, so I can't attend your lectures."

To this, the professor replied, "If you don't attend classes, I shall have no way of grading you, so just take a test."

Hideo took the test, and Professor Tatsuno said, "If you know this much, you don't need to attend classes."

There is another well-known episode, though I don't know how true it is. On a test given by the French literature professor Shintarō Suzuki, Hideo had written, "I refuse to answer such a foolish question." The professor proceeded to mark it zero.

At the next test, Hideo did so well writing on Mallarmé that Professor Suzuki scored it perfect, and reconsidered: "Perhaps that question on the previous test was foolish after all."

Professor Tatsuno had made available to Hideo books from his own library, which Hideo frequently borrowed, cutting out pages, circling and underlining portions at a time. When returned, the books had hair, dandruff, cigarette ash between the pages, which became Hideo's trademark, indicating that he had devoured the book. Professor Tatsuno, however, came to regard him highly, when he realized how voluminously and with what painstaking care he had read.

Chapter 12
People Value Feelings Most Of All

Reading the paragraph in Hideo's letter beginning with, "You are fortunate to have Takamizawa loving you so... ", I finally decided to marry Takamizawa.

Then a few days later, planning to send Hideo's belongings, I went to Takamizawa's place. He met me and said, "Everything's gone!" looking perplexed, and apologetic.

After we had carried Hideo's belongings to his place in Sakiko's absence, she immediately, on the very next day, carried them back to her house. She had taken back everything, leaving only a hastily scrawled note, "I'm taking Kobayashi's things back, Sakiko."

Keiko Matsumoto probably couldn't stop Sakiko from doing it. My heart sank, while at the same time I felt uncomfortable about Sakiko's abnormality—her stubborn unwillingness to accept defeat. I felt chills down my spine. Her persistence did not seem motivated by her love for Hideo but from a conceited unwillingness to accept defeat. I thought then her illness had turned for the worse after living with Hideo. She had realized her inferiority to Hideo, but her pampered, strong-headed conceit would not allow her to admit this.

Giving up on her, I told Takamizawa about my feelings, and we decided to marry. Then we went next door to Keiko Matsumoto's, and explained that Sakiko had taken back Hideo's things and that we planned to marry.

Keiko, always gracious and helpful, put aside Sakiko, and took delight in our plans to marry. She, acting as our go-between, offered to go the next day with Takamizawa to the Yanaka house to obtain my mother's approval.

My spirits dropped at her offer. I knew my mother would not disagree, but I understood her innermost feelings. She was insecure—being widowed and long plagued by poor health, lacking any savings for old age and finding Hideo irresponsible. She had wanted me, at least, to marry someone of some means, a secure job, and a future—this I could understand. Takamizawa, however, was insecure, lacking any savings or a stable job and, as a cartoonist, had an uncertain future. I was saddened that my marriage fell far short of my mother's expectations.

That night I told her about my plans to marry Takamizawa. She said nothing.

Already in July, I had written to Hideo about how Sakiko had reclaimed his things, so I could not forward his Western clothes, but would send kimonos instead and a mosquito net. I also wrote that I had decided to marry Takamizawa, and asked him to write a magazine article. At the time, Kunio Kishida, Toyoo Iwata, Hideo Nagata, Jirō Sekiguchi and others had founded a New Drama Study Centre, where I had been going. They planned to publish the magazine *Higeki Kigeki* (Tragedy and Comedy), and had requested that I ask Hideo to write an article for it.

His sixth Kansai letter, a postal letter card, arrived with "Japan Postal Letter Card" printed from right to left at the top and with an oval three-sen stamp on the left. It was postmarked 13 July in Nara.

> Fujiko,
>
> Thank you for the postcard. I don't need my Western clothes. I haven't bought a mosquito net because I ran out of money. Please send me some.
>
> It's hot and uncomfortable every day. I want to form the habit of getting up early, but I don't wake up until noon. It's so hot I can't do anything until night.
>
> I want to write something big, so writing a short article is somewhat a nuisance; but I will, if possible. I have no idea what kind of magazine Kishida is publishing.
>
> It's better not to remove my belongings from Sakiko's.
>
> So the ceremony is set for September. I'm sure you two will be happy.
>
> People value feelings most of all. Don't worry about the daily thoughts you hold, but rather the daily state of your heart. The same holds true when seeing things. The important thing is to see with the heart. If you want to write novels, continue writing. Unless one writes with what lies in the heart, one can never write anything worthy.
>
> Can you send me about five yen? I did some shopping and ran out of money. I can't ask Uncle Shimizu for more until the month's end.
>
> Please send me the kimonos too.
>
> My regards to mother and Takamizawa.
>
> Hideo

I repeatedly read this postal letter card, particularly the words, "People value feelings most of all" that followed "So the ceremony is set for September." Hideo wrote these heartfelt words, words that had received a painful but noble baptism. By the word "feelings", he probably meant love, sympathy, tolerance, flexibility, kindheartedness and empathy for others, which I believe are central not only for married couples but in all human ties.

Thanks to Hideo's advice prior to my marriage, I have enjoyed a long, successful marriage. Of all the advice he has given me, I have been most influenced by his words "People value feelings most of all" that are long buried in my bosom. Thus, whenever I write or speak on Hideo, I have particularly quoted over and over these words of his.

Undoubtedly, after leaving Sakiko and living alone for three months, he finally realized that his nightmarish life with Sakiko had actually enriched him as a person.

Also, the words in his letter "I want to write something big" most likely refers to his manuscript of "Various Patterns", which won a prize from *Kaizō* magazine the following year. After being deeply hurt, Hideo was on the road to recovery by July and had immersed himself in writing the manuscript.

Also he had written an article on Valery's "Shigaku" (Notion of Poetry), as I had requested the following year (1929) in March for publication in *Tragedy and Comedy*.

Each time during this period that I received Hideo's letters I felt more relieved. By then, I felt Hideo had finally recovered.

About a week after I had received his 13 July postal letter card, I went to Yato to see Keiko Matsumoto, and then Takamizawa. I had just entered his house but before I could speak Sakiko came running up. She desperately wanted to talk with me. I felt my heart beating rapidly as I stepped out again.

We went to the opposite side of the lot and talked as we walked round and round the tennis courts, with the hot summer sun shining obliquely upon us. It is over fifty years ago, and I have forgotten the details, but she repeated many times over that my hand-copied letter shown to Keiko had been fabricated. She claimed that Hideo could not write such a letter and that he would eventually return. I answered her repeatedly that I had not deceived Keiko or her, that the letter was genuine and that Hideo would not return. She absolutely refused to believe this. Of course, she never made the effort. She was the most obstinate person I had ever met. Thinking it futile to convince her, I gave up.

I felt then I understood what Hideo meant by "[she] lacks heart". She lacked any desire for affection and also the humility to admit that she wanted Hideo back. She remained indifferent and aloof to her faults.

Hideo had for several years agonized over her. He had failed disastrously to relate to her, which exhausted him so that even holding a pen was unbearable. But Hideo had recovered marvellously well and had begun writing again by mid-July.

Hideo once told me during one of our sake drinking evenings at his mountain-top house: "I never look back. In regard to my life and writing, I always think ahead and look forward. Once I complete something, I only feel the urge to contemplate a more difficult task."

From his higher school days, Hideo had always felt the urge to find a deeper, more challenging, more exacting task. Then he plunged himself fully into achieving this end. The writer Ukichirō Nakaya once said, "Rare is a person like Hideo Kobayashi who so willingly expends his body and soul without the least regret." This was Hideo's strength. It enabled him to lift himself from the nadir of life.

Shichihei Yamamoto, a well-known writer, wrote, "No matter to what length I read Kobayashi's writings, I see no sign of 'a complaining face'." But I believe this characterized all his writing, his words and attitude to life. This outlook of Hideo—never regretting how much mental energy he expended—never for a moment allowed him to despair or complain. He was too preoccupied with the present to do so.

Hideo often yelled at, cut down, swore at and emotionally bruised others, but he never spoke behind others' backs, or snared them in traps. When drunk on sake, he raised his voice, speaking ill of and criticizing people's actions, but only to enlighten; he was never offensive to people if they were present. Even on matters difficult to speak about, Hideo spoke frankly, but he never spoke behind their backs. He had an optimism, I believe, that was rooted in his deep honesty and sincerity. He absolutely could not lie!

Why did Sakiko fail to see this sincerity in Hideo? Perhaps she was incapable because of the sickness revealed by her abnormal behaviour, as Hideo stated, "[she] lacks heart".

Added to this abnormality, she had probably become senile by the time of her *Bungei* magazine interview "Memories of Hideo Kobayashi" (1983). For this reason she also made serious errors in her brazen accounts of Hideo, which I have previously corrected. But when I am reminded how Hideo himself did not lie, I can no longer remain silent about her false account. Hideo's wife, Kiyomi, also remarked how she pitied Hideo when she saw so many reading Sakiko's article. Sakiko may have believed her account to be true, but her memory had gone to seed. She makes errors about the years things happened and the places where they happened, and her stories are farfetched.

Sakiko's account is harmful, so I have attempted to give an accurate account of what Hideo said and did. People misunderstood Hideo since he rarely explained himself or made excuses, but Sakiko's fabrications only open the door to new misunderstandings. I must repeat that "[she] lacks heart" in her interview account. And I make clear here that—aside from her mysophobia, which she may have recovered from—she still remains abnormal. This makes her impossible to deal with.

She errs in so many places that I must limit myself to correcting only the most blatant cases in the order that they appear in the article. The first concerns the time Hideo abandoned her:

> I shouted, "Get out" and he went out. Though he parted with his clogs sounding in the distance, I thought he would return, but he never did. The very next day, I went to Dangosaka, because his mother and sister lived there in a rented house, and inquired about him. When I was told that he hadn't appeared there, at first I thought they were concealing him. When I said he had left me, they said it was probably because I had nagged him so much (laughter).

What make-believe, how wrong this is! At that time, my mother and I lived across from Yanaka Cemetery near Nippori Station, and Sakiko had never visited that house. Nor had she ever met my mother there. Granted she may have confused Dangosaka for Dōsaka—we did not move to Dōsaka (in Takinogawa near Tabata Station) until more than six months later.

She claims that she met me by chance at Hakusan, the diviner's place, to whom she said I went seeking my brother's whereabouts. But I have no such recollection. Whether his name was Hakusan or not, I have forgotten, but I did go once to a noted diviner. A university student at Kunio Kishida's New Drama Study Centre had offered me the free services of his uncle who was noted as a diviner. Plagued by my own problems at that time in late 1926, and with Hideo moving about with Sakiko from Kamakura to Zushi, I had no one to confide in. Since I had not become a Christian, I went to the diviner to inquire about my future fate. This was over a year before Hideo had abandoned her in 1928, and I had gone only to consult the diviner about my own problems. I had no reason to visit a diviner at the time, since Hideo had already notified me of his whereabouts.

After I had sent the kimonos, a mosquito net and some money to Nara as he requested, his letters to me stopped. Some weeks had lapsed since walking around the tennis courts with Sakiko in late July. Then I received a letter from Hideo in September, one page in length, filling the back of a 400-character manuscript sheet.

> Fujiko,
>
> Thank you for the kimono the other day.
>
> I have just returned from Wakayama. I thought of writing from there, but the daily swims fatigued me so. I hardly felt like holding a pen.
>
> Since returning to Nara, my life has been the same. But it's autumn already. The air shines with the mountain hues with the change of

season. The mating season is approaching, so the bucks will soon be dangerous. Every year, people are killed by their antlers. However, no one needs to fear if one is careful.

Is everyone well? I wrote something for the September issue of *Bungei Shunjū*, so please forward the money to me.

I certainly took it easy this summer. It was so hot.

Now I feel that I can write. My mind is full of ideas, but I feel I have a gap to overcome before I can begin writing.

Life in Nara is monotonous but truly peaceful. I have no need for adventure for a while.

My regards to mother.

Till next time,

Hideo

Hideo had gone to the coast in Wakayama prefecture and had acquired a dark suntan as he had swum there daily. Though still penniless, Hideo was certainly enjoying the springtime of his youth.

Chapter 13
One Can Study And Create Art Under Any Circumstances

I am not certain how long Hideo stayed at the Nichiren Temple in Osaka, perhaps for ten to eleven days, but as soon as he received the kimono I sent him he went straight away to Uncle Shimizu's in Kyoto. Always straightforward, Hideo most likely hid nothing when he revealed to Uncle Shimizu why he had left Tokyo. Apparently impressed by Hideo's frankness, Uncle Shimizu took his predicament to heart and had Hideo stay at his house for four to five days early in June. After that, Uncle Shimizu had Hideo stay in a nearby inn, since the household was in commotion over the divorce of his son, Keichan. Aunt Shimizu in particular was distressed.

Hideo, who found refuge there, had written the letter to me by brush on Japanese stationery at Uncle Shimizu's. The copy of *Tannishō* that he had read and sent to me, Uncle Shimizu had given him from a shelf of his bookstore. I can almost visualize Hideo browsing through some books on Buddhism and immediately reading one that had particularly caught his attention.

Hideo's appetite for reading had returned as his last paragraph of this letter, pencilled in red, indicates.

> Please send the following books from the Yanaka house [where my mother and I then lived]: *Chronique de Canard Sauvage* (by Charles Louis Phillipe) and *L'Éve Future* (by Villiers de l'Isle-Adam).

It was during his three or four days at the inn, I believe, that Hideo found within the Kasuga Shine precinct in Nara a detached hut at the Edosan Restaurant, where he decided to live. The one-room detached hut was evidently old and in ruins. Hideo, however, enjoyed the small place: the rent was very cheap, and he was surrounded by the quiet, bountiful richness of nature's beauty.

Freed from a hellish life with Yasuko, he found he was nourished by nature's beauty in the carefree, relaxed life he spent there. Deer wandered up to the hut and he found Nara's lush greenery a special treat. Oblivious to his poverty, Hideo submerged himself in nature, freed from any thoughts of the future.

> Every year at about this time, I think of Nara during this season. Though Nara's lovely, verdant greenery cannot compare with that of Kamakura, at no other time have I so completely forgotten everything and inhaled the scents of the green leaves. Though I had just graduated from university and was wandering about like an emaciated beggar, how exhilarated I felt in spirit! I was on my back under a beautiful cluster of wisteria, feeling that I had just seen a dream of two thousand years. No matter where, one cannot find such clusters of wisteria hanging in that way.
>
> *(Asahi Weekly Magazine,* 1929)

When Uncle Shimizu invited us to go sightseeing in Kyoto and Nara four years earlier in 1924, he arranged for us to spend a night at Uncle Nishimura's at Yamashina in Kyoto. Uncle Nishimura had taken us then to see the Miyako Dance in Gion, but he had moved to the southern suburb of Osaka in Suita by the time Hideo settled at the Edosan detached hut in 1928. It was there in Suita that Hideo dropped in on him unexpectedly.

The first son of Uncle Nishimura, Kōji, was a student at Kwansei Gakuin University, and the second son, Teiji, was a middle school student. On this occasion Uncle Nishimura took Hideo to see a play, asked him to tutor Teiji in mathematics and had a photograph of the three taken together. It shows Hideo wearing an unpressed summer *yukata* with a black sash, while concealing the back part of his hair that Teiji described as growing thick and wild.

The author Naoya Shiga lived in Nara at the time, not far from Hideo's hut. Shiga too had requested that Hideo tutor his son—probably to provide a small income for Hideo. Thus, Hideo came under the wing of Naoya Shiga, perhaps troubling him in no small way.

Since his middle-school days Hideo had held Naoya Shiga in high esteem: perhaps because Naoya had praised Hideo's maiden work *Suicide of the Octopus* (1922). Actually, Hideo had read Naoya's works from much earlier [i.e. before 1922] and highly respected him. Much later in life, Hideo would sip sake out of a broad, yellowish tea-bowl made by Bernard Leach, one of Naoya's favourite bowls, which he had given to Hideo as a keepsake. Hideo would hold it tenderly, gaze into the bowl and slowly sip sake from it. Each time more than likely he reminisced about his days in Nara, unable to forget his great mentor throughout his life.

Hideo first met Naoya Shiga in 1921, the year he entered First Higher School. He received advice from Naoya then, which he put into practice. He used to say that this advice stayed firmly in his memory because it turned out to be true. What Naoya said to him was:

> When one is young like you, one can never be too proud. It is just right to have a little too much pride then. A time will come when circumstances don't allow you to be so.

Following this advice, Hideo resolved not to fall behind anyone when it came to pride. When Hideo couldn't understand something, he was so conceited that he believed it was a major event. Then during his Nara days, he lost this capacity for pride.

Soon after Hideo arrived in Nara, his cousin Kōji Nishimura visited him. He mentioned that his university's literary arts club intended to invite a lecturer from Tokyo. Immediately Hideo said, conceitedly, "It will be a boring lecture! Tell them as a committee member of the literary arts club that inviting a lecturer from as far as Tokyo isn't necessary. If they invite me, I'll guarantee them an interesting lecture. I may be unknown, but I have a graduated with a Bachelor of Literary Arts. You must invite me! Of course, I'll expect a lecture fee."

With a grin, cousin Kōji left. About a week later Hideo received a telegram, "Request you to lecture." This surprised Hideo. It was good news, but he lacked the train fare and a suit. He possessed only the one worn-out, serge kimono he had on his back. Troubled, Hideo rushed to Naoya's with the telegram in hand. Naoya, at a loss, requested Hideo to go try on his father's old suit, now in the possession of the writer Kōsaku Takii. Hideo went to Takii's house, but when Takii brought out the old suit—blue and magnificently homespun—it fit like a potato sack on skinny Hideo. Normally unconcerned about appearance, Hideo realized this time that this baggy suit would cause laughter to rain down upon him as he mounted the lectern.

Hideo remained in low spirits, then Naoya's young nephew Noboru visited from Kamakura to do some painting in Nara. He wore a suit that Naoya spotted and said to Hideo, "Try on his suit."

Hideo did and found it a perfect fit. It had no vest, so Hideo borrowed the vest from Takii's baggy, homespun suit. This being the only mismatch, the audience probably would not notice and burst out laughing. He borrowed some shoes, a watch, a fountain pen and train fare. Now satisfied, he returned to his hut. On a postcard he scrawled, "I accept the lecture offer", jotted a title like "Realism and Symbolism in Literature" and posted it.

On the day of the lecture, Hideo approached the front gate of Kwansei Gakuin University where he saw a large billboard that read, "Realism and Symbolism in Literature—Hideo Kobayashi, B.A." It was Hideo's first public lecture. Feeling uneasy and in need of a boost, he retraced his steps to a bar to have a beer and then returned. Facing thirty to forty students, he started to speak but lost track of his conclusion as the alcohol took effect. Looking at his watch, he saw he had spoken for two hours and fifteen minutes. Then, saying, "I do not wish to speak too long on a subject that has no limits", he crisply bowed and stepped down from the lectern. Cousin Kōji met him, saying, "I couldn't make head or tail of the lecture."

Hideo received his lecture fee, and went directly to nearby Kobe to wander around, then the next day to Osaka. He spent a week in Osaka drinking in the noted Dōtonbori nightclub area, when he chanced upon a former drinking acquaintance and caroused about. Afterwards he made it back to Nara and returned the suit.

Hideo's article, "Shojo Kōen" (First Lecture) (*Ōru Yomimono* Magazine, December 1940) gives this account, and ends with:

> I finally returned to Nara. On the way to Naoya's to return the suit, I came to Sagi Pond, where I spotted a young man painting in a white shirt and shorts. It was Noboru.
> When I extended my apologies, he retorted, "I couldn't go anywhere without my suit."

It was an essay, and so Hideo sometimes exaggerated for the sake of humour, while at other times he omitted things and adlibbed. Though Hideo wrote in the Monthly Supplement accompanying the *Collected Works of Hideo Kobayashi* that he didn't return the suit for a week, Noboru writes that he received it three days later.

As he says:

> I got my suit back safely enough, but I believe Hideo did this sort of thing all the time to his friends.

Hideo inconvenienced many around him everywhere he went.

Osamu Kimura, a former First Middle School classmate and member of the Crescent Mandolin Club who later became a drinking friend of Hideo, relates what Hideo had omitted in the story of the suit. While drinking in Osaka's Dōtonbori area, Hideo quarrelled with some ruffians, who proceeded to heave Hideo off Shinsaibashi Bridge into the river below, where he broke his front tooth. I don't know how true the story is, but I believe him capable of engaging in such a fight. When he drank, Hideo became argumentative, so I believe he did scuffle with those ruffians.

Even ten to twelve years later, he involved himself in similar mishaps that almost cost him his life.

While Hideo lay critically ill, I didn't expect him to actually die. I had expected he would live another four to five years. I was deeply saddened since I had wanted him to live. A few years before he had said, "At least, I'll take care of my health and live a life fitting for an elderly person."

In his fifties and sixties, Hideo did not think about ageing. In his essay "One's Sixties" (1962), he writes, "I live according to what my age dictates", without mentioning his age in years.

Only at the age of seventy-five or seventy-six did he talk about ageing, but I never considered him old until the day he died. His white hair, rounded shoulders and stiff movements indicated that he was old, but he never aged in spirit. His face was alive, his voice was clear and crisp and once he began talking on any topic, his viewpoint was always invigoratingly fresh. To the end, I felt in him a vigour that remained youthful and forward looking.

Ms Masako Shirasu, a good friend of Hideo, wrote an essay on Hideo in an evening edition of *Asahi Newspaper* in 1983. She wrote humorously: "To me, he was a sour old man.... Though he is dead now, he still remains a sour old man," perhaps because Hideo had sternly criticized and often reprimanded her. Never thinking him an old man, I found her comments strange. He was old in age, but I felt in him a youthful power, which was not due entirely to my partiality as his sister.

Because I felt this way, I could not accept his death, which I regretted as premature. However, before his first memorial service in March 1984, I re-read about Hideo's life in his youth and also some of his essays. I concluded that a lifespan of seventy-four or seventy-five years was perhaps appropriate for a person like him. Only his concern for his health a few years earlier, or perhaps even before then, had enabled him to prolong his life to a ripe old age of eighty.

I said, a person like him; this, of course, cannot be explained in a few words. That is, from his primary-school days he possessed a superb mind and keen intuition, and read voraciously. His avid reading influenced me immensely. In the four-and-a-half-mat room facing north with my tiny desk adjacent to his, I tried my best to read as he did, but his books far surpassed mine in difficulty even though he was only two years older. I was engrossed in girls' novels, whereas he was reading Jun'ichirō Tanizaki's short story "Ningyo no Nageki" (Lament of a Mermaid) in *Chūō Kōron* which so impressed him that he was beside himself with joy. At the time he had just entered middle school. He re-read this novel so often that some ten years later as a new literary critic he could repeat the opening paragraph. Once in middle school, he went through works by authors such as Dostoevsky, Tolstoy and Turgenev, published at the time by Shinchō Publishers in small, translated editions.

Not limiting himself to reading, once in First Higher School he began to write for a coterie magazine, and completed his virgin work in his second year, the novel *Suicide of the Octopus*, which was later, praised by Naoya Shiga. He also enjoyed drinking and carousing. He became critically ill, and fell deeply in love the year he entered university. He took his love affair seriously, so much so that he exhausted himself physically and emotionally. This led to untold suffering for mother and me, which also deprived Hideo of any joy. His university years became the most difficult of his life.

Hideo wrote afterwards:

> My university years were most trying. In an interview with the student editor of *University News*, I vaguely thought that I had never read the *University News* during my time at university. Tormented by my self-imposed alienation and illusions, I had not the time to read it. In fact, I had no time at all to think of university life. I lacked the time even to go to buy a student uniform. This may sound strange, but, slowly reflecting on it now, I realize that I never wore a uniform because I didn't have the time to go and buy one. I had nothing against uniforms; if I had been given one I would have worn it. In spite of this, some may say that I did well to find time to graduate, but I did so because I lacked the courage to disappoint my mother, who was looking forward so much to my graduation.

Though tormented by Yasuko's illness and often unable to attend university, Hideo's unique behaviour left an indelible impression on his classmates. He rarely attended classes but apparently always appeared when the Frenchman Albert-Claude lectured on Racine. Even Shintarō Suzuki, later an honorary professor of French literature at Tokyo University, who didn't know Hideo at first, heard from Professor Tatsuno of an astute student named Kobayashi. Later Suzuki read Hideo's written test paper and was deeply impressed by his brilliance. Student test papers were normally kept in the university office for two years and then burned, but the professor found Hideo's paper too good to burn and kept it in his study, ignoring the school rules. Professor Suzuki had forgotten about it, but remembered some forty years later when Hideo received the Cultural Achievement Award. Elderly then, he stripped off his shirt on a hot summer day and searched for the paper, wanting to re-read it. Behind a stack of books reaching to the ceiling, he found a bundle of papers wrapped in yellow paper with the years marking Hideo's university days. As a lecturer at the time, the professor had assigned the topic "On Mallarmé's Prose-Poem 'Demon of Analogy'", the intent and interpretation of which had long eluded even the best of scholars.

Thus after some forty years, Professor Suzuki re-read Hideo's paper and wrote of being deeply moved at Hideo's fresh and original interpretation, not available even in France. At the end of his paper, Hideo had added, "Sorry to hand it in late", indicative of his youthful innocence.

After the note, Professor Suzuki had pencilled in red a comment, "Extremely interesting. Unconcerned by its lateness, I enjoyed reading it."

He later humbly admitted these were unnecessary comments.

For Hideo, these university years were the most trying emotionally and financially. He was tutoring the writers Shōhei Ōoka and Tetsutarō Kawakami, translating for others, writing fill-in articles and publishing anonymously "Aruchuru Ranbō Den" (The Life of Arthur Rimbaud) and "Sharuru Bōdoreru" (The Life of Charles Baudelaire) in *Bungei Shunjū* magazine. Given his adversities, it was amazing that he had managed to write such an outstanding test paper. Moreover, he had his thesis, "Arthur Rimbaud, Dogmatist" (now called "Ranbō I"), as the sole creative article published in the first issue of *French Literary Studies*, edited by the university's French Study Centre. Hidemi Kon had first suggested its publication, and he was enthusiastically supported by Professor Tatsuno. The articles were mainly written by senior teachers, with only a few by students, but Kenzō Nakajima claims that Hideo's article stood out.

In his university years, Hideo not only worried over Sakiko's illness but also struggled to make ends meet and missed classes. Nonetheless, his keen mind was in full throttle, plunging into research, thinking in depth, and writing a remarkable paper. Furthermore, his youthful purity had led him to apologize for the late paper.

As a result of this experience Hideo believed firmly that, "One can study if one must, and create art under any circumstances if one sets one's heart on it." He had faced near defeat in a state of emotional ruin, but nonetheless maintained a spirit filled with passion that enabled him to create a writing highly original and valuable.

Chapter 14
Don't Let Anyone Know

In May 1928, the year Hideo graduated from Tokyo Imperial University, he freed himself of Sakiko and went off to wander in Osaka. Concerned about his whereabouts Professor Tatsuno met with his students Hidemi Kon, Masaaki Satō, and Kenzō Nakajima at the French Literature Study Centre. Professor Tatsuno said: "Yesterday's evening paper reported a car had run over a man in Kasukabe [now, Kasugabe in Saitama prefecture], he might have been Kobayashi."

Hearing this, the three students telephoned the *Yomiuri Newspaper* office, rushing there to inquire further. No one there could allay their concern until the poet Chūya Nakahara appeared and explained to them the real reason for Hideo's disappearance. He, however, had no idea of Hideo's whereabouts.

Hideo had sent me a letter in June so as not to worry mother. But he had strictly ordered me not to tell anyone of his whereabouts, and I faithfully obeyed and kept it secret.

After three hellish years with Yasuko, Hideo evidently wanted to be alone in the Kansai region without meeting anyone. To heal his emotional fatigue, he was seeking a life free of cares and desires, roaming about as he pleased. He nonetheless was forming his basic literary thoughts during those months.

Ideas for his award-winning essay "Various Patterns" (1929) had taken shape during his vagabond days. Also, his thoughts on the illusion of music, later included in his essay "Mozart" (1946), were taking bud.

Long after he was established in literary circles, Hideo continued to seek perfection. Always true to his feelings and himself, he probed deeply into each idea, cherishing each truth and seeking spiritual development as he tackled each painstaking task.

In time, people came to call him "divine", "founder", "genius" and so on, but no one, including his closest friends, understood him, I feel. In one sense Hideo was always a loner.

Shichihei Yamamoto wrote that Hideo did only what interested him, saying and writing only what he wanted. He was greatly blessed and fortunate as a man who loved life. He bought what he wanted even though he couldn't afford it and did as he pleased, despite causing problems for others.

He enjoyed his unheeding ways that at times almost cost him his life or brought him injuries in his younger days. In addition, he twice considered taking his life in periods of mental agony.

A person who lived as recklessly as Hideo could not be expected to live a long life. Perhaps this is what I am trying to persuade myself of now.

In September 1928, I married Takamizawa, who moved his possessions into the Yanaka house. We lived there with mother for a year and a half.

Then about mid-October my mother, who rarely left the house, decided to travel to Kyoto and Nara to personally thank uncles Shimizu and Nishimura, Naoya Shiga and others for looking after Hideo. She had wanted to go earlier, but decided that a time after the hot summer had passed and after my marriage to be more appropriate.

It took a whole night on a sleeper those days to reach Kyoto, and her first long trip alone worried my mother, who was in poor health. Takamizawa and I went with her to Tokyo Station to see her off; we helped with her bags and numerous gifts, but I felt sorry for her. Whatever house she visited, she would have to express her gratitude, apologizing and bowing deeply. I did not despise Hideo to the extent I did earlier, but, nevertheless, I resented his bringing mother additional sorrows and burdens.

After about a week's visit in Kyoto and Nara, she returned, quite fatigued, and reported that Hideo finally wanted to settle in Tokyo and write. Also, mother had told him that before her departure to Kyoto Yasuko had won the "Miss Greta Garbo Resemblance Contest" sponsored by a newspaper, which could gain her a movie contract with Shōchiku Films. Of course, mother reported all the details and events of her visits in Kyoto, but I can only recall the above. Her trip was not all distasteful, since she met new people, enjoyed some interesting talks, took in some sightseeing, and visited the detached hut at Edosan, perhaps even spending a night there with her son. Thinking back on these possibilities, I now try to comfort myself as I reminisce about her.

We had decided it best that Hideo live with us in Tokyo until he could make a living by writing. We searched for a larger place and found a two-storied house in Takinogawa, in Tabata (now Kita ward). The Western-style artist Misei Kosugi (Hōan Kosugi), founder of the Shunyō Society, lived next door to us then.

Soon after we moved in, Hideo finally returned to Tokyo from Kansai in 1929. That first evening we four—Takamizawa and I, my mother and Hideo—went to the Ginza to dine, and drank sake to celebrate Hideo's homecoming.

He lived about three years at the Takinogawa house except for about a month when he lived in Chiba to write his essay "Various Patterns".

The book *Tabata: Town of Literati*, published by Kōdansha Press in 1975, lists Misei Kosugi, Hideo Kobayashi and Suihō Tagawa (my husband's pen-name) as noted residents there. However, in those days, Hideo and my husband were unknown. Misei Kosugi, our neighbour-artist, who had two live-in maids, would hardly grant us a face-to-face meeting when we made our courtesy call. The book, however, relates that the Kosugi household had taken notice of us, the maids envying our cosy, new married life. It mentions also that Sakiko approached our house but, characteristic of her, she stood hesitatingly outside, when the sight of me leaving the house frightened her off.

That summer Hideo completed his essay "Various Patterns", which he submitted for *Kaizō* magazine's writing contest. Again, Hideo exuded his youthful pride, as Naoya Shiga had advised him to in Nara. Confident of winning first place and the prize of three hundred yen, he asked a friend to advance him the sum, with which he bought some books, although he spent most of it on sake. This was before the announcement of the winner.

He was placed second, not first. The second prize sum amounted only to half the first prize, which left Hideo bewildered for some time.

Nonetheless, Hideo had grounds for his confidence, since the judges had heatedly debated the first and second place winners, the final vote ending in a deadlock. In the end, it was the proletarian writers who constituted a majority in the group that placed the essay "Haiboku no Bungaku" (Literature of Defeat), by Kenji Miyamoto, first.*

Nonetheless, we celebrated Hideo's winning second place when the four of us—Takamizawa and I, Mother and Hideo—went again to the Ginza. This and the occasion I mentioned previously were the only times that the family dined out together. This notwithstanding, my mother found this simple banquet in the Ginza perhaps the happiest and most memorable event of her entire twenty-five years of widowhood that began in 1921. On this night my mother, though thin and frail, filled her bosom with the highest hopes for Hideo's future, enabling her to momentarily forget all her hardships and sufferings of the past.

Soon after, as usual, a life of loneliness and insecurity awaited her until her death in 1946.

Having feasted to the full, we strolled along the Ginza when Hideo entered the elegant Shiseido Cosmetic Shop without saying a word. We followed without intending to make any purchase, but then Hideo bought me a small bottle of perfume. It came as a total surprise, as it was so unlike Hideo to

---

* Kenji Miyamoto later became the chairman of Japan's Communist Party.

buy me such an expensive gift. I was overjoyed especially since I knew he owed money on his prize money. I thought that he had bought it as a belated wedding gift, which he couldn't afford the year before. Holding back my tears, I pressed the box of perfume close to me.

Hideo's first essay, "Various Patterns", was published in the *Kaizō* magazine in September 1929; this finally established him in the literary world. In October, he became a member of the *Bungaku* magazine coterie and began publishing his series of translations of Rimbaud's "Season of Hell". In December, he published in *Shisō* magazine the essay "Naoya Shiga". Then from April of the following year (1930), he began writing his series of "current criticisms" in *Bungei Shunjū* magazine and, in October, published his first book, *Season of Hell* (translations), with Hakusui Publishers.

Soon after moving in to the house at Takinogawa, Suihō Tagawa (my husband) saw his work flourish too, and eventually Kōdansha Publishers contracted him to draw most of the cartoons for its magazines. Many people visited those days at the Takinogawa house: editors of magazines, friends of my husband and Hideo, and also student admirers of Hideo who aspired to be writers. In March 1929, the year Hideo returned to Tokyo, I resigned my position at the girls' school but retained three tutoring jobs, which often kept me away from home and meeting Hideo's visitors. Among them apparently were Shizuo Fujieda and Ken Hirano, who came together to visit him. Those days when Hideo was busy writing, he stayed aloof from the family members, except for occasional drinking sessions with my husband. Also, at that time Hideo was downcast and kept to himself, wrote Ken Hirano who, seeing this with Fujieda, at once felt obliged to cut short his visit.

On one visit Hideo saw Fujieda out of cigarettes and opened the closet to give him a pack. Hirano was surprised to see the closet full of Bat cigarettes.

In those days Hideo smoked numerous packs of Bat cigarettes, now the Peace brand; they were the cheapest and had the most nicotine. In addition he drank heavily.

Ken Hirano writes about the gloominess and poorly lit rooms of the two-storied Takinogawa house, which actually did have little sunlight and poorly arranged rooms. Nonetheless, in the three years at this house, the careers of both my husband and Hideo took bud, and found a niche among the major publishers in Japan.

While at this house too, my husband Suihō Tagawa had begun in 1931 his now famous cartoon series "Norakuro" (Stray Dog Blackie).

Chapter 15
I Had Failed To Repay My Mother For All Her Love

It was from age of twenty-two that Hideo's good fortunes changed, the Asakusa diviner had told Hideo.

The fact is, however, that the entire family's fortune had plummeted after father's death in March 1921, when Hideo was nineteen. Soon after, in September, our mother coughed up blood, whereupon she moved to Kamakura to recuperate. Though I was traumatized, Hideo was deeply affected, aware that the family was in debt and that the responsibility was his as the eldest son. Perhaps for this reason, he fell critically ill that October and nearly died.

In 1925, at the age of twenty-three, Hideo entered Tokyo Imperial University but soon fell into an intolerable love affair, which brought a torment hitherto unknown to him. He had brought this upon himself and assumed the burden of this despair. Although the diviner said his good fortunes had reversed, it had left an undeniably positive effect as well that moulded and matured his character so as to enrich his later writing.

Believing in divination or fortune-telling sounds absurd today, but my mother reared in the old Meiji tradition had long suffered poor health and, as was typical of girls those days, was never taught to have a life of her own. Thus, she found herself believing in character-trait omens, name-omens and fortune-telling, having no other firm religion to rely upon when faced with problems.

My mother once said that on seeing Hideo's face a diviner had predicted, "This child will successfully do something never before accomplished." My mother long believed this, holding great hopes for Hideo, which were, however, cut short when she passed away in May 1946. Hideo had showed great promise as an established literary critic but had to cease publishing during the war years from 1941 to 1945. Some claimed that the news media had "black-listed" him. In spite of this, soon after my mother's death, a leftist literary group accused Hideo of being a war supporter, as a member of the Unification Movement. He, however, had severed ties with the Patriotic

Association of Japanese Literature during the war. Disgusted with opportunistic writers and the militaristic media, he had retreated into a world of his own. Hideo writes of those days:

> The literati are being requested to lend support by stirring war sentiments, but we literati are aware of only writing. So, if I should be drafted, I'll put aside the pen, take up a rifle, and go to the front.

My mother died soon after, so I believe she did not die happy as she was denied the pleasure of seeing the diviner's predictions of success for Hideo fulfilled.

While our father was still alive, our mother occasionally attended the women's meetings of the Jōdo Shinshū sect. I remember accompanying her several times to see the famed beauty Takeko Kujō and to hear Entei Tomomatsu, who was noted as an eloquent speaker on Buddhism. I had returned home impressed by Mr Tomomatsu's passionate talk and Ms Kujō's beauty. However, when our father died and mother fell ill the same year, she cut her ties with Jōdo Buddhism entirely.

During my mother's recuperation in Kamakura, her maid was a believer in Tenri-kyō. Thus, Tenri-kyō priests visited mother at home, explaining that only her *ki* or spirit and a change of heart could cure her. Their kindness and humility persuaded her to believe in Tenri-kyō. Mother and the maid would sit before a small altar placed in the alcove and chant repeatedly the lines, "Almighty Tenri of Life, bestow upon us help..." as they waved their arms. My brother and I saw this every time we visited her.

When our mother returned to Tokyo in 1924, we moved together to Mabashi, Kōenji, in February, where a neighbourhood Tenri priest visited occasionally. But after she and I moved to Yanaka, Nippori, in 1927, she lost contact with Tenri-kyō.

Though mother was religious, she was frustrated in her ability to fully believe. She was also frustrated in her inability to understand Hideo and his lonely torment during his youthful years, but she depended on her only son far more than on me. I too found Hideo inscrutable, until after the time he left for Kansai and explained everything in his letters to me. Both mother and I angrily resented Hideo, ever since the time he had travelled to Ogasawara and Ōshima islands in 1925 when we were in dire financial straits.

Some forty years later Hideo told me about his Ogasawara trip: Hideo and two others went from Hachijō Island to Chichi Island, then on to Haha Island where the rain forced the boat to dock. This forced them to stay there for several days, left with time on their hands. Finding no available inn, they stayed in a boarding house where they ate fish and huge shrimps that were tasteless even after being fried. But Hideo found the coral reef island, surrounded by white sandy beaches and the clear blue ocean, inviting.

To pass the time, the three went mountain climbing, but became lost. Finally, they made their way to the coast by evening. There they came upon a shack where they found rice, *miso*, pots and pans. Tired and famished, the three decided to spend the night there. They cooked the rice and boiled some pumpkins from the garden and added sliced sugar cane. Later, they inquired about the man who had lived there and brought him a bottle of sake to thank him, but this was unexpected, so the owner thanked them apologetically.

Hideo describes this in his essay "Kikō Dangen" (Travel Tidbits), which describes that final eerie night spent in the shack. It was undoubtedly an eerie night, which I feel alluded to the agonizing thought of suicide that lingered in Hideo's mind.

Between 1930 and 1931, Hideo published essays in almost all the major literary magazines such as *Bungei Shunjū*, *Shinchō*, *Chūō Kōron* and *Kaizō*, and published books one after another. He thought his success now enabled him to live in a rented house, so he moved with our mother in November 1931 to Kamakura.

In Kamakura, Uncle Moku and Aunt Wakana Jōya had lived in a house next door to our mother during her years of convalescence from 1921 to 1923. They had tended to mother by constructing a passageway that connected her house to theirs, with a door installed at the property line through which she visited regularly. During vacations, both Hideo and I often visited the place in Kamakura, staying up to a week during summers to enjoy daily swims. Even since the early 1920s, Kamakura had been a place familiar to us.

When at university in the late 1920s, Hideo lived about six months in Kamakura with Sakiko, from where he commuted to Tokyo University. By the time Hideo made Kamakura his home with our mother, numerous literary people had settled there, including Masao Kume, Seijirō Kojima, Fusao Hayashi, Kyūya Fukuda, Kensaku Shimaki, Jirō Osaragi and Hidemi Kon. Hideo liked Kamakura, and I, too, thought Kamakura's benign climate beneficial for our mother's health.

However, mother opposed moving to Kamakura. She admitted that Hideo deserved his own home, but she thought they should live near the Takamizawas in case of need. One reason was that she desired to live near her only daughter, but another was that Hideo was often absent from home. He used to disappear for weeks at a time when we lived at Mabashi and Takinogawa. It was good then that I happened to be near her on those occasions. This time she dreaded being left alone with Hideo in Kamakura.

About that time, I remember Hideo taking my mother to Uncle Moku when they were house hunting in Kamakura. He left her there, and went on to see Hidemi Kon. Purportedly, he went to request Kon's help to find a rented house and then return. But after some talk, the topic changed, whereupon he drank, they tossed a ball between them, and finally he spent nights there. After a week there, Hideo remembered, "Oh no! I came to Kamakura with my mother and left her at Uncle Moku's. I forgot."

Hidemi Kon said Hideo hastily returned. Hidemi related this episode in his farewell address at Hideo's funeral.

Such was Hideo's nature that my mother naturally feared living away from me and Takamizawa.

Then finally they moved to an old house on Sasuke Street in Kamakura. I went to help them move and spent that night there, but found the house unhealthy for mother, for there was very little sunlight. Hideo began searching for another house saying that it was overly hot in the summer.

Soon he moved near Hidemi Kon's house in Yuki-no-shita, next door to Jirō Osaragi, where I went to help him again. This time the house, built sturdily as a villa, had rooms well laid out, abundant sunlight, and a large yard. On the day of the move Kon came to assist, and then again on later occasions, which my mother appreciated. When feeling better, of course, she did a little work, wiping the pillars and doors with soap and hot water or pulling out the weeds in the yard. Hidemi took Hideo and our mother up to Mount Kamakura, which she described, to me in a letter.

> What scenery. How refreshing the scene to see Enoshima Island and Enoshima Sea all at once and Mount Fuji immediately in front. Let's go up there together. A branch Tokyo hotel is here which has dancing, and we can have meals here. It's high up the mountains, so it's a bit chilly rather than cool....

This time, from late autumn 1931, Hideo increasingly absented himself from home. Once, as a good son, he had purchased two kabuki tickets to treat our mother to her favourite outing. But two days before the performance he disappeared, failing to return by that morning. I received a call from mother then, asking me on short notice to accompany her.

At times she would be in bed, overworked or with a cold, when in deep loneliness she would write to me.

> I occasionally feel well, but not always completely so, which I find a problem. I prepare my meals a little at a time, but the pains in my hips and my legs trouble me. Now a month has passed, so I am feeling depressed....You two are planning to visit here at the month's end, which I look forward to more with each passing day. As you know, I am often alone here, so, my daughter, your visit will be a welcome treat. Come as soon as you can, and spend some time here. Stay

overnight. My letters may sound like complaints but I have no one else to talk to, so I talk to you, my daughter, by letter....

Your brother, as usual, is out. I suppose that, tiring of taking strolls in Kamakura, he often goes to Tokyo. He has gone out three times this month already and spends the nights away from home. Two days ago, as soon as he woke, he left and he has not yet returned, though it is almost 8 p.m. Since I do not feel well yet, I ask him to return soon. I beg him to return, but he only replies, "Yes, I know", and he does not return. Forgive me for spilling the same complaint to you year after year, but I have no one to talk to, so do so by writing to you, Fujiko. When I write, I can momentarily forget my loneliness....

My body feels dull, and I have headaches and pains in my hips and back, and dizzy spells; I cringe at the thought of doing anything. Since I am alone, I cannot recover my health. Hideo spent four days in Tokyo, and returned two days ago at 1 a.m. But as soon as he got up yesterday morning, three acquaintances came after him to go flower viewing. He didn't come home last night either. I don't know whether he will tonight. I am not very well, and Hideo is so often out. If I am such a nuisance to him, I believe I must change my frame of mind. I don't feel like sewing, which is my favourite pastime. I merely sit before the charcoal brazier, absent-mindedly waiting for the sun to set. After the sun sets I make supper, eat and go to sleep. This is my daily routine. Because my hips hurt, I want to take a hot bath, but I am unable to haul in the water to prepare the bath. The bathhouses are about five long blocks away, too far to walk. I dreaded moving here to Kamakura, but Hideo promised to mend his ways so I came, but he hasn't changed a bit. Now I regret ever coming here. If I were in Tokyo, I would find so convenient the natural gas and running water. I get dizzy spells carrying water every morning and evening.

When my mother was confined to bed, Uncle Moku's maid came to prepare meals for her, but now that she was on her feet again no one came to lend a hand.

Including today, your brother has been gone six days. Please forgive me for writing about my complaints again. Alone, gazing into the charcoal brazier, I have become disturbed, realizing how all thoughts seem so bleak and dreary.

Hideo was somewhat aware of mother's health and insecurity but once he set himself on a certain task, he simply forgot all else. His mind was involved only in that one task, which he toiled over. But his single-mindedness brought problems not only to mother, but to all those associated with him. No one was an exception. Though he left my mother alone, Hideo truly had her on his mind. Hideo had expressed his concern verbally during unguarded moments—Hideo's closest friends spoke of his filial piety and concern for his mother. My mother mentions this concern in her letter.

> Your brother returned last night. Though it was late, I asked him to prepare a hot bath. My hips feel much better today. Perhaps because of the improved weather, I'm in better spirits. Now I will go to mail this letter and try walking a bit.

In 1946, the year after the war ended, when we all lacked daily needs, my mother passed away after a period of illness. Hearing by phone of her death, I rushed from Tokyo to the Kamakura home, where waiting anxiously Hideo met me at the entrance. Then tears began to fill my eyes.

The hot sun reflected against the crematorium, which looked quite dilapidated. Hideo clutched close to himself the urn, wrapped in white cloth, into which my mother's ashes had been placed. The tenderness with which he embraced the urn expressed his grief so well.

Even twenty or thirty years later, Hideo used to say to me, "I was irresponsible as the eldest son. I failed to repay my mother for all her love."

Chapter 16
"Norakuro" Will Remain

In 1932, the year after Hideo moved to Kamakura with mother, Meiji University founded the Literary Arts Department and appointed such lecturers as Kunio Kishida, Tatsuji Miyoshi, Hidemi Kon, Hisao Tanabe, Seiichi Funabashi and Hideo himself. All of these lecturers were unique in the way they conducted classes, but Hideo was by far the most notorious.

Without hesitation, he broke university rules and didn't organize his lectures, which gained him the reputation of being irresponsible. This was perhaps more unpardonable than leaving an ill mother unattended at home.

Smoking by teachers in the classroom was strictly prohibited those days, even during off hours. Ignoring all such rules, Hideo would drop himself into the lectern seat upon entering the classroom and light a cigarette. Then leaning his chair against the blackboard he lectured puffing away at his cigarette. Before long, both his feet would be propped on the lectern desk. He never stood during his lecture, brought a textbook or lecture notes, and always rambled on as he pleased. All these earned him a "notorious" reputation. Still students found his ideas so profound and creative that they were left deeply impressed.

He assigned one test a year, a paper on unusual topics such as "Know Thyself", "On the Genroku Period" or "Afterthoughts".

He lectured on the literary arts, but then one day explained: "I am bored with teaching what I know, so I'm going to start teaching on a topic I'm unfamiliar with. What's wrong with teaching something I don't know well?" So he began lecturing on Japanese history. In this period he studied Japanese history, which later benefited him both personally and in his later writings. In fact, I believe his teaching Japanese history during this period greatly helped him to write his last major book, *Motoori Norinaga* (1977).

One day reflecting, he said that he had often entered the wrong classroom and begun to lecture. I said, "How can a teacher be so disorganized?"

He answered simply, "I'm not the teacher type."

He wrote much and even lectured at Meiji University to earn enough to support himself and our mother, but he was always short of money. Most of his income he squandered on drinking, dining and carousing, which left mother financially wanting. She wrote to me concerning her worry about paying the rent. In another letter, she explained that she needed the fee to get the instructor credentials for which her flower-arrangement teacher had qualified her. This credential would provide her some confidence in teaching. She requested that I ask my husband to lend her the money.

In another letter she wrote that Hideo did little at home, often cancelled classes and often absented himself from home. However, this was characteristic of a period in which his writing led to intense writing sprees throughout the night.

After one and a half years at Yuki-no-shita, Hideo and my mother moved to 391 Ōgigayatsu in 1933; a small inn with a mineral-spring bath was located a few minutes' walk from the house up the hill. Named Komeshin, the inn was actually a "lovers' rendezvous" inn where, after an exhausting night of writing, Hideo would spend the entire day.

The back-washer boasted that Yoritomo had once bathed there in the mineral bath, but the inn had long lost popularity and had no guests in the daytime. In the vacant bathing room Hideo would recline as the sunlit spot provided sweet comfort.

It was here that Shōhei Ōoka and Tatsuji Miyoshi later stayed.

Hoping that Hideo would marry and settle down, Uncle Moku and Aunt Wakana in Kamakura, as well as mother, introduced young girls to him. mother wrote about this. A mother and her daughter visited and had supper with them, and afterwards the four of them strolled along the coast to Hase Kannon Temple and the Great Buddha, then parted. Or, through an introduction Hideo went to Nara to meet another girl. My mother thought some girls recommended by acquaintances to be ideal for Hideo, but not being satisfied, he declined.

She writes at the end,

> We took pains to introduce several girls to him, but Hideo claimed mother was unable to find anyone to his liking, so I'll keep quiet and let him find someone himself.

So until his marriage in May 1934 he led an absolutely carefree life. He writes about his life in his essay "Names Identical" (1945):

> Speaking of newspaper articles, I read one reporting that a Hideho Kobayashi passed away. I had not met him, but while teaching at Meiji University I had heard of a teacher named Hideho Kobayashi in the Preparatory Course. Since I lived with my mother, I had a permanent address but slept wherever I fancied. I often went to Meiji University after a night at a *geisha*-house in Asakusa. I failed to appear there for a

while, realizing I could not pay my debts. Then the *geisha* house complained to the university to the great embarrassment of Hideho Kobayashi. I heard of it later and was embarrassed.

During this period Hideo was a prodigal son who neglected family duties and university regulations, but his lectures and notable writings exhausted him body and soul.

He also participated in sports at the time. Opposite the rear of Kamakura Station, he played tennis at the courts there or played baseball with other writers gathered at the oceanside field. One summer at the 391 Ōgigayatsu house, where I visited intending to spend a night, Hideo invited me. "Today, we're going to play baseball, so why not come and watch."

It was hot, but I climbed onto a small truck with Jirō Osaragi, Hidemi Kon and others to watch them. Hideo played catcher and surprised me when he so intently chased after fly balls, sometimes falling head-over-heels. Hideo certainly exerted himself wholeheartedly. Whatever he liked, he enjoyed thoroughly. Good writing perhaps requires such a trait, as an older writer commented:

> He wrote, drank, and womanized when a young man and brought money problems with him, but it was admirable how he thoroughly did as he liked with such headstrong determination.

During this period, I went to the 391 Ōgigayatsu house whenever possible to spend the night with mother because I felt sorry for her. I also sent her Kōdansha magazines that published my husband's cartoons or some sweets, and I took her beef extract (an imported and expensive, nourishing health drink). I invited her to visit our place. She was delighted to spend a night or two at our apartment in Koishikawa.

We had found the Takinogawa house too big for us after Hideo and our mother moved out, so my husband found an apartment in Matsuzumi, Kanda, a studio-type one. It had one Western-style room with a double bed, and a kitchenette. At first, the double bed was a rare treat, but we found the single room inconvenient, so we soon moved to another apartment on a hill at Koishikawa, Kuzeyama, near Kōdansha Publishers. It had a three-mat and six-mat room, and a small kitchen.

To this apartment I often invited mother. We played mahjong with a newly married woman next door, a Japanese-speaking German housewife. Sometimes I took mother to the movies. By these means I tried to comfort her.

However, I could not blame only Hideo for living a carefree life and leaving mother alone at home. She, perhaps in her ill health, unnecessarily brought worries upon herself. She cast a gloominess and saw herself as more unfortunate than need be by perceiving all matters so pessimistically and hopelessly.

Nonetheless, in this predicament Hideo maintained a sense of purity.

My husband and I had started mountain climbing and skiing, since life in our new apartment allowed us the time. Hideo too loved the mountains. Once, in his third year in middle school, he and two others had got lost attempting to go from Kumotori to Mitsumine. Running out of provisions and not knowing what to do they luckily came upon a fisherman who helped them. Whenever we talked about mountain climbing, Hideo always wanted to join us. However, with mother and us two eking out a living, we could ill afford the three- to four-day trip to Japan's Northern Alps. But we often invited Hideo to the nearby mountains. We made the first climb to Mount Tsubakuro. It was a real climb those days, on foot from the foot to the peak with no roads like today. Next we three went to Mount Hodaka and Mount Yari.

Before boarding the train, we bought some fruit at Takano's Fruit Shop in Shinjuku. I bought some inexpensive sour summer mandarin oranges, much more sour in those days than they are today. Hideo bought for us ten wrapped Western pears that were rare and expensive. Although I thought he had spent too much, I gladly accepted them as we boarded the train. Rather than the sour mandarin orange, I wanted to taste the Western pear and peeled one. It was edible but too ripe and soft, and not sweet. Except for one or two, Takano fruit could not have all been bad, but Hideo had taken one bite and said, "It tastes terrible. It's too ripe. It's better not to eat any."

Thinking this wasteful, I wanted to try peeling another one, but Hideo disposed of the entire pack in the rubbish bin, ashamed at having bought such over-ripe fruit.

I strangely remember this incident so well. A lovely sense of purity impressed me when I saw his disappointment as he disposed of his gift as soon as he found them unpalatable. He had purchased them at great expense from his limited money.

After spending the night at Kamikōchi Highlands, Hideo cut across to Mount Hodaka with a guide, while the rest of us climbed to Mount Yari and returned before nightfall. When we reached the lodge, Hideo had not yet returned: he finally came back as we were about to finish supper. Hideo explained how a fearful thunderstorm had delayed them and they had barely escaped death when lightning struck a nearby boulder.

Soon after, from around 1931, Hideo proceeded to climb numerous mountains with Kyūya Fukada, who had interested Hideo in skiing by teaching him. Other members of the literary group had also taken up skiing, going to such areas as Ike-no-daira and Akakura. Masao Kume, Matsutarō Kawaguchi, Hidemi Kon, Tatsuo Nagai, Mosaku Sasaki and his wife and a close physician friend at Keiō University also joined them. We Takamizawas went as well, on the invitation of Hideo. We skied and fell all day—and ate, drank and partied like innocent children at night in the large straw-mat room.

Setting up a swimming race on the straw-mat, we pretended to dive on top of it on our bellies, racing ahead in the crawl and butterfly strokes. Masao Kume performed the Tokyo *ondo* dance; it was truly a pleasurable night.

The day of 9 April 1933 marked father's thirteenth memorial service. It had been postponed for some reason from the usual date of 20 March. At that time father's grave was located at Seifukuji Temple in Shi-no-hashi in Minato ward on the trolley-car street, but it was relocated in 1977 to near Hideo's home at Tōkeiji Temple. After the Buddhist ceremonies, we attended the supper held at Nakajima Japanese Restaurant, located in a side street of the Ginza. Guests included only close relatives, certainly Uncle Moku and Aunt Wakana of Kamakura, Uncle Saburō who continued father's work, and Aunt Yūko of Shirokane. Our uncles and cousins who had taken us touring in Kyoto, however, were unable to attend.

Mother left for home early, going with Uncle Moku and Aunt Wakana to Kamakura. And soon after this, Hideo, my husband and I left to go to another Japanese restaurant named Iwadeshinobu to which Takamizawa often went. It had been converted from a charcoal dealer shop. The storage room once piled high with charcoal had been cleaned, renovated and redecorated into a straw-mat restaurant. It had a certain atmosphere, which was a bit too gloomy for me.

Takamizawa had been occupied with the now popular cartoon series "Norakuro" since 1931 and had not drunk leisurely with Hideo for some time. This time they both drank freely and talked until they were quite drunk. The subject turned to "Norakuro" when Hideo commented on some cartoons, "In ten years cartoons by others—'Rakuten', 'Ippei' and 'Kunibō' —will fade out, but 'Norakuro' will somehow remain. The caricature of 'Norakuro' is wonderful. You've created a great motif."

This made me happy and I replied, "Maybe so, but I can't take you seriously in your drunken stupor."

Hideo retorted sharply, "The drunker I am, the keener my mind. I can perceive much better. This includes the feelings of others, so don't look down on drunkenness."

Ten years later the war hysteria brought cartoons to a halt just as Hideo had predicted. Noted cartoonists had to cease drawing and some had passed away. "Norakuro" too came under censorship, leaving Takamizawa with no work.

The war ended in 1945, after which he gradually resumed his "Norakuro" cartoons in magazines, but they failed to regain their prewar nationwide popularity. Some said that the press claimed Suihō Tagawa as a wartime casualty, or printed his name as the former Suihō Tagawa. Some commented to his face, "So you're still alive, are you?"

These comments made Takamizawa utterly despondent. It was then that Hideo told him, "A genuine work will never die. 'Norakuro' is genuine."

This simple comment uplifted my husband in no small way. Only Hideo had encouraging words for him. Takamizawa later said in joy that this had uplifted him as never before.

My husband knew that Hideo never commented for the sake of flattery.

Chapter 17
Criticism Without Love Is Amiss

Hideo's predictions proved true in many instances, including his comment to Takamizawa: "Something genuine lasts, and 'Norakuro' is genuine." Comic books saw a resurgence in publication from 1971—forty years after "Norakuro" had first begun as a series in 1931 in *Youngsters' Club* (Shōnen Kurabu). Within four or five years, ten volumes had been reprinted and read nationwide by adults in their forties and fifties who were nostalgic for the comics they had read in their childhood. Children joined fathers in reading them, some becoming new fans of "Norakuro" though they found the prewar orthography somewhat difficult to read.

Adults nostalgic for "Norakuro" founded Norakuro clubs throughout Japan, including the Tokyo, Osaka, Nagoya and Hokkaido areas, from which Takamizawa continues to receive invitations. In addition to the ten reprints of originals, Takamizawa illustrated five new volumes under the title "Norakuro, Continued" for publication to meet new demands.

At last, my brother found a girl he liked, my present sister-in-law Kiyomi, whom he married in May 1934.

Prior to their marriage, I had met her once when Hideo and our mother moved to the house at 391 Ōgigayatsu in the spring of 1933, their home for over a year. When I visited the house, I saw Kiyomi, whom Hideo very briefly introduced to me as I served them tea, "This is Kiyomi Mori. Kiyomi, this is my younger sister."

Hideo said nothing more, indicating an explanation was unnecessary. Neither did my mother mention marriage. Perhaps such talk was still premature, but I intuitively felt it.

After they decided to get married, Kiyomi often visited the Ōgigayatsu house. I knew little of the details. Evidently her father angrily opposed the marriage, perhaps afraid that he would be left without an heir. In this unsettling situation, Kiyomi made several trips to Matsumoto city in Nagano prefecture to persuade her father. After a long time she received his permission.

In the 1930s, few wedding ceremonies and receptions were held in hotels as they are today. Only Meiji Shrine and Gajoen Hall in Meguro had such facilities for weddings in the Tokyo area.

Both of our uncles had held their weddings at home, because our father disliked ceremonial formalities. When Uncle Saburō Jōya married in 1924, only the person acting as the groom's father, closest friends and relatives were invited to their home in Tokyo. The bride's younger sister and I made most of the preparations and arrangements, except for a catered meal. Next, Uncle Moku Jōya's wedding also consisted of a simple exchange of nuptial cups, which took place at their Kamakura house. Only close relatives attended this and a small reception.

Hideo also probably resented the formality of a marriage ceremony before a Shintō or Buddhist altar, but he acceded to our mother's request as he did for his university graduation ceremony.

They also invited only a handful of relatives; the small number did not require the printing of wedding invitations. Mother wrote them with a brush in her name and Hideo's. The Takamizawas received the following handwritten invitation:

> Our warmest appreciation for your help the other day. Hideo's wedding ceremony will be held at Gajoen Hall in Meguro at 2:20 p.m. on the 6th of next month. We request your attendance hoping it will not inconvenience you in your busy schedule. We express our gratitude for your most lovely gifts received yesterday.
>
> Yours lovingly,
> [Signed by Hideo and Mother]

Jirō Aoyama and his wife served as the go-between couple. Mrs Aoyama was the well-known *jiuta* dancer Han Takehara. She arrived early in her Japanese *marumage* hairdo and crested black kimono, but the central figure, Jirō Aoyama, failed to appear. We all waited anxiously, until finally the Gajoen Hall attendant requested a substitute go-between to keep to the schedule, whereupon Uncle Saburō was designated. On such short notice, in front of the Shintō altar he stumbled over the words as he read the marriage vows written by brush on a large, thick sheet of paper.

The ceremony had already ended and the reception begun when Jirō Aoyama appeared in a crested *haori* and *hakama* skirt. Without any formal greeting or acknowledgement of the guests, he started to drink sake and get drunk with Hideo. Just before the end of the reception, they left and disappeared into the night.

After such a disorganized ceremony, I feared the hardship and loneliness that Hideo would bring his new bride as he had to our mother. He had often left her alone though the two lived together. But this worry was unwarranted.

He had taken two to three years to find his genuine love, and he truly cared for her. He took her to many places. In January the next year, in 1935, he took her skiing, perhaps because I suggested it. They went skiing somewhere every month that winter though they were usually accompanied by literary friends. In January they went to Kazawa, in February to Sugadaira and Nozawa, in March to Kanbayashi and Kusatsu. Together they enjoyed their amateurish skiing.

In the beginning, of course, his bride scolded him, complaining that he drank too much and came home late at night. Occasionally these escapades of Hideo's resulted in arguments, but this occurred in our marriage as well. But later, after the marriage of their daughter Haruko in March 1965, they became much closer, the two left to themselves.

Early in the marriage, however, whenever immersed in his writing, he neglected his wife as he had his mother. Lost in his work he forgot all else, including his family, although he was a father to his child and a husband concerned about his wife. Once she came to understand this trait in Hideo, Kiyomi quietly initiated her own interests. She spent many hours reading, as she learned to trust and rely on Hideo.

Left to themselves after Haruko's marriage, Hideo often asked Kiyomi to accompany him on walks or visit interesting places that he had newly discovered around Kamakura. Once he took her to an old temple, perhaps the ancient Raigo Temple, where she mentioned the beautiful radish flowers had recently bloomed. He took her out to lunch, or to see items of interest. About one-third of the time Kiyomi declined, not wanting to dress up each time or not feeling up to it. At such times, Hideo went alone.

After Hideo's death, she expressed endearingly, "Why hadn't I joined him more often when he invited me? How I regret it now."

On travels, particularly in his later years, she always accompanied him. Prone to motion sickness, she had long refused to get on a plane, but finally began to fly to Ōita prefecture in Kyūshū and enjoyed her travels with Hideo.

As for travels earlier in their marriage, Hideo often invited Kiyomi and Haruko to Kyoto or Osaka for sightseeing when he lectured there. Much later, Hideo related to me that in 1939 he had gone alone to his lecture and then arranged to meet Kiyomi and Haruko at Kyoto Station. The Kyoto trip then took nearly a day without the services of a super-express train.

"What a terrible time I had. The locomotive came to a stop, and I waited and waited, but they failed to come out on the platform. Thinking it strange, I looked through the windows searching for them and at last spotted them—both were fast asleep!"

Apparently in those days trains made long stops. I laughed heartily, but Haruko replied sharply, "That's unfair. He says we were both asleep, but I was a baby, one year old or so at the time. Why shouldn't I have been asleep?"

Kiyomi felt deeply for Hideo. After Hideo's death in 1983, she offered incense and flowers before a large portrait of Hideo. But unable to bear looking into the true-to-life face, she replaced it with a smaller photo showing his profile instead. Also, Haruko and I eagerly listened to the records and taped cassettes of Hideo's lectures when they became available. His familiar voice sounded so close to us that it newly aroused grief in us, for this reason Kiyomi still refuses to listen to them. She fears his voice will remind her of his death, a thought too painful to bear.

Kiyomi, Haruko, his grandchildren and also his close friends all felt the depth of Hideo's love. Hideo was an affectionate person; he expressed affection even for his writing. Writing involved many painstaking moments, but he held dear affection for his writings. Like Chekhov, Hideo's affection ranged from people to life itself.

Hideo married Kiyomi in 1934, a period when most Japanese men discriminated against women to a degree unimaginable today. Few women were allowed to ski, especially as husband and wife. Kiyomi and I, however, were fortunate. Indeed, many Japanese writers are esteemed for their insights on humanity, and they regard women as equals. But others in their daily lives still dominate women, using such disparaging terms as "you women folk". Hideo found such condescending remarks disgusting, an opinion he later expressed in his essay "Joryū Sakka" (Women Writers; 1938).

> A writer like Chekhov, so calm to appear almost strange, avoids such aphorisms as "you women". For example, he writes in a letter, "I detest fellows who either praise or disparage women, since neither man nor woman are worth a cent."*... Writers of great literature do not write as man or woman. Their writing requires a foolishness like Chekhov's. To be a writer, one must not write as a man or woman. The writer's soul—that is, the poetic soul—is a strange entity that grasps some aspects of man only after destroying it.... In many intellectual endeavours, not only in literature, women have begun to equal men in ability and talent. This is good, and man must guard against interfering with the progress of women.

Since early in his career, Hideo regarded both men and women as compatible and equally worthy of love—as equals in weaknesses and foolhardiness.

Hideo always said, "Criticism without love is amiss," insisting that criticism be centred on love.

---

* From the Japanese translation.

About the same year, in 1939, Hideo wrote a criticism of Ms Masako Ogawa's book *Kojima no Haru* (Spring on a Small Island), which had impressed me as well, for *Asahi Newspaper*. The following excerpt appeared on the dust jacket.

> Of the books read recently, Masako Ogawa's book *Spring on a Small Island* is most impressive.... I... hope that many such books will follow and that the public will read them. By such books, I mean not those in which the writer avoids lies, but those not requiring creative writing. The writer of these memoirs need not attempt to record everything accurately. Her heart is so filled with truth, she doesn't have time to invent lies. Such a human record affords most interesting reading even for the world at large.... This woman's soul glitters with wholesome wisdom, which overwhelms me. Doing away with sentimentalism or stubborn logic, this writer's flexibility of soul is not limited to that of a woman doctor. This writer succeeds in truly educating, so that it would amaze the best of educators participating in an education symposium should they read the book.

Reading only this reveals Hideo's deep search for truth and his endearing love for this writer who lived truly in self-sacrifice for her patients.

Hideo began writing *Mōtsaruto* (Mozart) three or four years before mother's death; it was finally published in December 1946, the year of her death. Though this was only six months after our mother's death, Hideo admits that its overtones surprised even himself. He says that the grief in *Mozart* most likely expressed that regarding his mother's death, which had compelled him to dedicate the book "To my mother's soul".

I have treasured the 1949 edition of *Mozart* he gave me. It was published by Nissan Publishers, a volume 1.3 cm thick, of B6 size and with a cardboard case. Though it is printed on the best paper available during the postwar years, it does not compare in quality to paper today. The crimson cover bears the title "Mozart" in gold leaf and the flyleaf is thick, brown Japanese paper. The decorated title page comes next, followed by the dedication page inscribed with "To my mother's soul". All the pages are bordered in thin, brown lines in number 4 large Minchō typeface.

The words of dedication move me, as does the large print that brings tears to my eyes. Since it is a short work, naturally only a large print could make it book size, but I feel, nonetheless, that Hideo requested a large print to enable mother to read it with her fading eyesight. So each time I open the book, I sense Hideo's endearing love between the pages. This edition, I believe, is the most priceless among Hideo's books—for me and all readers.

It occurred in August the year mother died, during the old Obon Festival dates. It was only a year after the war, when the unrepaired Suidobashi

Station platform was rickety, dangerous after the wartime bombing. Late one night Hideo, dead drunk, tripped and fell ten metres to the street below the station, holding onto a large sake bottle. When he regained consciousness, he heard a man's voice saying, "He's alive, he's alive", and felt a hand checking him for injuries. He was carried to the stationmaster's room, and the next day transferred to the office of Sōgen Publishing Company nearby in Kanda. Kiyomi says she almost fainted when she received the news by phone, certain that Hideo had been seriously injured. Fortunately he had only suffered some bruises and hairline fractures of the ribs. However, until we heard the hospital report we were quite worried. He was in good spirits when four or five days later I visited him at the hillside Ōgigayatsu house. He announced while sitting up in bed that he would soon go to Yugawara hot spring in Izu Peninsula to recuperate.

I said, "You probably escaped serious injury, because in your drunkenness your body fell limp."

He answered in all seriousness, "Perhaps so, but I think it was Mom who protected me." Then he left for a fifty-day rest at Amanoya Inn in Yugawara.

He described this incident many years later in one of his "Kansō" (Afterthoughts):

> Apparently the large sake bottle I was holding shattered against the side of the concrete road, covering me with bits of glass. As I lay atop the black coal cinders, and looked at the bits of glass reflecting in the streetlights, I concluded that mother had saved me. That moment, I did not think or feel that mother had saved me; I definitely knew she had.

Chapter 18
A Kind Heart Is One That Feels

In 1948, Hideo purchased and moved into a large, single-storey house on the mountain slope behind Hachiman Shrine. The climb was taxing, but the elevation of the house provided it with luxurious surroundings. The landscape was magnificent, the mountains filled with the beautiful changing colours typical of the four seasons. In spring, fluffy-white mountain-cherry blossoms covered the mountain greenery, and autumn brought yellow-brown-crimson tinted leaves to weave a brocade on the slopes. Towards the southern horizon, the view was of the blue ocean and Ōshima Island, which could be seen distinctly on clear days. I was told that at night the spraying lava called the "goddess fires" of Mount Mihara could be seen.

Although Kamakura as a popular tourist spot hustled and bustled with tour buses, cars, motor scooters, student excursions and throngs of walking tourists, once I reached it, Hideo's mountaintop house stood as a quiet haven. With each visit, I felt my soul and body sink into a blissful rest.

The large yard included a pond and a lawn, big enough to allow Hideo to practice his putting when taking a break from writing. The entire house was typically Japanese, except for the study and sitting-room, which were soon remodelled in a Western style to make the house more practical.

A successful businessman previously owned it, but died soon after building it. His widow moved out with her two small girls to a smaller house and decided to sell the large house. The two girls, about the same age as Hideo's daughter Haruko, often came to play with her. In sympathy for the bereaved family, Hideo looked after them like his own daughter.

Thereafter, Hideo lived in the house for almost thirty years from 1948 to 1976. As the two girls grew in age, they came not only to visit but also to help and house sit. They frequently spent the night, so I often met the girls there, and we enjoyed supper together.

Hideo concerned himself about their future. He referred the younger sister to Kadokawa Publishers, where she found employment in editorial work. Health reasons prevented the elder sister from work, so Hideo asked me to "arrange" a marriage partner for her. I managed to find two or three prospective husbands.

In 1954, she finally married the Reverend Kanoo Naitō of Morioka city in a wedding at Yuki-no-shita Church in Kamakura. Hideo and Kiyomi attended the wedding, where Hideo happened to be seated next to Dr Hidenobu Kuwata, President of Tokyo Theological Seminary, who invited Hideo to speak at the seminary.

Known for his sincere, acerbic, but humorous lectures, Hideo was often asked to speak but invariably he declined. He has written:

> For some reason I don't like to lecture. I have often lectured, but never on my own initiative, since I place no trust on the effectiveness of lecturing. I cannot express my innermost thoughts in the form of lectures. My real work lies in writing, where I place all my joys and sadness.

Many approached me believing that at my request Hideo could be persuaded to speak, but he rarely agreed. He usually refused, even when I personally asked him on behalf of organizations that I belonged to. Three times he did accept: a lecture at the Tokyo YWCA, an interview for a Christian magazine, and the invitation from the President of Tokyo Theological Seminary. Though the President personally had invited him, Hideo did not at first accept. He finally agreed after I put in a request explaining the extent the President had helped the church I belonged to. A seminary student also made the climb to his mountaintop house to put in the same request.

He not only refused to speak at public lectures, but also on TV and radio. In spite of this, he agreed for a nominal fee when Aunt Yūko requested him to give a lecture.* It was sponsored by a small Buddhist group that she and Uncle Saburō belonged to. Hideo had felt indebted to them since his higher-school days. Out of an endearing sense of love, he never forgot about his obligations to those who had helped him. He did so genuinely out of a heartfelt desire to repay past favours. Also, Hideo frequently lectured and travelled on behalf of the publishers of *Bungei Shunjū*, since in his youth they had published his writings and moreover advanced him the money.

In 1955, one year after she married, Mrs K. Naitō returned to Kamakura from Morioka city for a week and paid Hideo a visit. She was about to depart for Morioka city from Kamakura Station. She told me that Haruko came to see her off and had given her a rare Western doll that she had admired since childhood days. She remembered crying with joy, assuming that Hideo had asked Haruko to give her the doll to comfort her as she returned to

---

* At Asahi Newspaper Hall.

the lonely Tōhoku district. After Hideo's death, she remarked to me that she still displays this doll.

In the 1960s, she and the Reverend Naitō were called to Kamakura to begin services in a private house. This led to a fund drive, by the 1970s, to build a church. I once asked the minister and his wife to obtain a large donation from Hideo and to convert him to Christianity. They hesitated in asking Hideo for a donation. But when I told Hideo of their low salary and the difficulty of their work, Hideo apparently responded, "I'll speak for him any time."

It was indeed rare for Hideo to offer to speak. Perhaps he still regarded Mrs Naitō as his own daughter, or he felt that he had attained the mountaintop house at the cost of the girls' misfortune.

The Reverend Naitō and wife were enthusiastic and planned for Hideo to speak at the commemoration service upon the completion of the new church. In February of 1981, a small but comfortable church was completed. They expected Hideo to speak at the church dedication service, but the following month, in March, Hideo was ill, hospitalized and operated on. A year later in 1983 he passed away without really recovering. Reverend and Mrs Naitō must have grieved deeply. At Hideo's wake and funeral service, both Mrs Naitō and her sister busily helped behind the scenes. Hideo would have deeply appreciated this, I believe.

During the years that Hideo lived in the mountaintop house, I used to go there, both to visit Hideo and to enjoy the house. I always had to rest along the way as I walked from Kamakura Station, and was breathless by the time I reached the front gate. However, once I entered the sitting-room, sat back on the sofa and gazed far out the window, I would feel renewed. Unobstructed on all sides by houses or buildings, the vastness of nature filled me with an indescribable sense of peace.

In addition, the sitting-room always displayed some of the finest curios and paintings available, which were a pleasure to see.

After he turned forty, Japanese curios as well as Japanese classical literature began to obsess Hideo, along with other items. When he lived on the hillside in the Ōgigayatsu house in prewar days, collecting pottery and ceramics, and paintings by Tessai and Sesshū had absorbed him more and more. Soon after moving to the mountaintop house in 1948, he turned to collecting an assortment of sword sheaths. Next he lost himself in old comma-shaped beads. Removing them from a small copper case after undoing the purple silk cord, he often showed me their various sizes and colours. I enjoyed looking at the emerald-like deep green stones called "ryokuchū", white crystal-like stones, and the beautifully curved deep green jadeite. These turned my mind back to Japan's ancient past.

Once something caught Hideo's fancy, he became possessed and probed until he unravelled its secrets. Once he felt he understood, he found another task that challenged his curiosity. He untiringly sought to understand the unfathomable, a characteristic of his "forward looking" personality.

I became busy in the 1950s, so my once or twice a month visit was reduced to only three or four times a year. Once I telephoned him the day before and made the hard climb up the slope to his house behind Hachiman Shrine. Hideo always did his writing in the morning, and in the afternoon read or finished the work. He kept to this daily schedule, so I usually arrived in the evening and had a leisurely supper. Since we talked at length while drinking sake, I usually spent the night there and left the next morning. On that day, too, I arrived well past 5 p.m. I can't remember whether it was spring or autumn, but it was a fine day.

Regaining my breath after the climb, I opened the large *koshi* gate to see Hideo in a kimono squatting before the front door, his head bent low, staring intently at the ground.

"Good evening," I greeted him.

Lifting his head slightly, he said, "Oh, hello," then continued to stare at the ground.

A small section between the gate and front door grew thick with moss, which Hideo was then collecting, though not as intently as ceramics and paintings. Whenever he found a rare species of moss on his trips, he inevitably brought a sample back to plant in front of the entrance to the house. Some of the many varieties rooted and spread rapidly, and others yellowed and died. A closer look at the moss might have been interesting, but I went straight into the house, since Hideo remained glued to the patch of moss.

A new oil painting had been hung in the sitting-room during my absence. It had replaced a painting of morning glories stuck in a German jug by Kazumasa Nakagawa.

At an inn in Akita prefecture, Hideo had seen a fan decorated with a beautifully coloured clematis of delicate shape and had asked Nakagawa to paint another oil with the same flower. Hideo waited for some five years. Then he asked for it again. Nakagawa apparently replied that he would send a painting of morning glories instead, unable to find clematis with inspiring colours as in the past.

The new painting on the wall, also by Kazumasa Nakagawa, depicted a street scene. Kiyomi explained it was a street in Pont-Aven in Brittany, France (where Gauguin had once lived). Attracted to this simple painting that made one feel clean, as if after swallowing a laxative, Hideo had purchased it at a Nakagawa exhibition.

As I was looking at it, Kiyomi said from behind me, "You know, Hideo played golf today, winning at long last. To celebrate his win, his friends invited him to a sumptuous roasted eel supper, but he came home early, saying that he was expecting you in the evening."

I felt bad about it. He had cancelled a roasted eel supper with his close companions for an ordinary supper with me; he had declined on account of his younger sister. Though I had telephoned the day before, he could have easily joined us later that night. It had been some months since we had seen each other, but postponing a meal together would not have been a great disappointment. Hideo however, had considered my feelings and kept his promise to have supper together.

A paper notice on the front gate cautioned, "During work hours, only those with appointments admitted." Hideo never saw anyone who visited unexpectedly without considering his convenience. However, once he made a promise he kept it, regardless how trivial, without the slightest fuss.

I knew about the roasted eel supper only because Kiyomi had told me, but Hideo made no reference to it. He did not mention having to make time for me, or the roasted eel supper.

However, the moss patch seemed to engage him more that evening; after thirty minutes Hideo finally came inside.

Hideo also loved animals and birds. Since moving to the mountaintop house, he kept a dog, though only a mongrel. Also birds often came prancing on his lawn, so he placed a nest box on a plum tree near the east veranda, and anxiously awaited the small birds to come and lay eggs.

I asked him, "What kind of birds would lay eggs there?"

"Japanese tits that come twice a year, and sparrows too. The sparrows, being stronger and bigger, turn away the tits. Sometimes, after a while, the tits fear returning. They leave in no time. As soon as the baby tits expose their heads from the nest, not fifteen minutes pass before they fly away with their mother."

Apparently, whenever the tits came to lay eggs, Hideo spent hours watching the nest box.

Hideo used to say, "Ah, when I sense beauty, how I feel love in time spent looking at flowers."

Also, he remarked, "Regardless of the knowledge and learning man may have, he cannot be a man of respect without a gentle heart, or one that feels."

Hideo was a man who feels. He was deeply sensitive to the human heart, beauty and truth. Thus he was considered a loving and kind man.

Chapter 19
One Truly Sees A Thing When Possessed By It

Hideo adored flowers too.

With flowers, however, Hideo showed a demonic intensity unlike the tenderness he displayed towards people and living creatures. He turned extremely volatile in terms of likes and dislikes. Also any item of beauty left him restless, in an uncanny state, until he had satisfactorily probed into and understood its secrets.

Hideo, in general, liked trees with flowers. With cherry blossoms, he became utterly obsessed; but he also liked plum-tree blossoms, camellias and andromedas. Flowering shrubs he liked too, such as rhododendrons, calabash and clematis. As for flowering grasses, he enjoyed delicate Japanese flowers like the traditional seven flowers of autumn including rape blossoms and Japanese toad lilies. As for most Western flowers—tulips, hyacinths, daffodils and pansies that some Japanese love to display in early spring—he disliked them. Even the prettiest of Western orchids, he usually shunned.

The gardens of his mountaintop house had four rhododendrons. Whether of the Japanese or Western variety, I forget, but probably the Japanese kind, since Hideo disdained Western flowers. Hideo eagerly awaited the rhododendron flowers to bud, but they failed to. Two or three years later, in the early '50s, finally one lonely flower with four or five petals bloomed, which Hideo studied gleefully like a child. Directly behind it an azalea bush was in full bloom with smallish, cute flowers.

After studying the rhododendron flower, Hideo walked through the front garden to the azalea bush, and proceeded to pluck off all the flowers. Kiyomi screeched in alarm, but Hideo said, "When looking at the rhododendron flower, the azaleas are distracting. How's that now. It's much better."

Satisfied, he resumed staring at the single rhododendron flower.

With a demonic sort of intensity Hideo pondered the beauty of rhododendron flowers. This uncanny persistence was typical of all his writings as well, and of the deep interest he took in ceramics and paintings until the 1950s. He once studied Tessai's painting entitled *Rokkyoku Issō no Daibyōbu* (Large Folding Screens of Six Paired Settings) for well over three hours.

Also, before the length of Sesshū's fifty-foot scroll *Sanzuihōkan* (Long Scroll of Mountains and Rivers) he had paced back and forth, and placed himself amongst the two figures in the scroll. He joined them in walking the path, climbing the hills, resting in the valley, and then gazing at the mountains and rivers. He had also gone to Mount Kōya to see the painting *Raigōzu* (The Coming of Amidabuddha), continually returning to the museum to lose himself for hours on end in that painting.

Someone wrote of Hideo that "[He had] the persistence of an alchemist, a rich aesthetic consciousness enough to fill any depth to the brim...." Of course, this persistence characterized all his writing; but, more noticeably, he would probe into an item of pure beauty to such a degree that a demonic look would appear on his face.

At the mountaintop house, spring welcomed the whitish-pink cherry flowers as they blossomed and dotted the surrounding mountains to weave a dream-like scene. In the garden, too, blossomed a magnificent double-blossom cherry tree. Called *fugenzō*, a rare variety, it had thirty-six petals (as actually counted by Hideo). The gardener surmised that perhaps none existed elsewhere. Hideo took pride in this *fugenzō* tree, which he treasured, and looked forward to seeing the beautiful blossoms each spring.

So ideally located, Hideo loved this mountaintop house. Intending to live there a lifetime, he had added a bedroom with windows facing south towards the sun. Actually he stayed about thirty years. As he aged, he began to feel its many inconveniences. It was too far to walk from the station, yet too near for cab drivers to accept him as a passenger to his house. The mountain path was also too steep for deliveries of grocery and for shopping, or for orders of prepared food to be delivered. But, in particular, he found the old spacious house difficult to heat adequately in the winter. Hideo, who hated the cold, struggled to keep the house warm. In the face of such problems, in January of 1976 he finally decided to move to a Swedish prefab house, a short walk from the main entrance of the Hachiman Shrine.

In particular, he wanted the double-blossom cherry tree to be transplanted to his new home, but the gardener advised him that the tree would fail to take root. Fortunately, Chōzō Yoshii, Hideo's good friend and new owner of the mountaintop house, understood and invited Hideo and Kiyomi to view the full blossoms in spring while having a festive meal. This became an annual occasion.

Cherry blossoms delighted Hideo; he decided to see all the famous cherry blossoms in Japan. He often related stories about them to me. He had gone to see the cascading cherry-blossom tree at Miharu, Fukushima prefecture—a National Memorial of Nature—in April 1972. He explained his wonder at seeing the deep purple blossoms of the reddish drooping variety, which apparently were in full bloom around 25 April. Hideo said that the tree was

600 years old, but the photo-postcard that pictured the beautiful blossom dated it as being 1,500 years old. Deep purple, the blossoms swept down like a broad waterfall that hung like a steady flow of water. Hideo was concerned, however, that the influx of tourists would damage the tree's beauty after five or six years.

He also told me about the *usuzumi* cherry blossoms, in the National Memorial of Nature at Neodani, Gifu prefecture. He had sent a telegram requesting the date of full bloom before he went. Being 1,200 years old, it had once nearly died, he said. Then a concerned elderly physician brought in a nurseryman who dug around the tree and planted some 200 young cherry blossoms where they camped during the nights. After this effort, the ancient tree survived to continue blooming to this date.

Hideo also described his trip to Kakunodate in Akita prefecture to see the drooping cherry blossoms in the yard of someone's house. Next he mentioned the cherry blossoms at Hirosaki, Aomori prefecture, that he saw in 1963.

> The cherry blossoms at Hirosaki Castle were spellbinding; great crowds came to see them. However, next to the trees, a magnificent cultural building has been built—where exhibitions and music programs are held, and scholarly lectures with commentators are provided. Most visitors went thinking these to be cultural, but I believe those travelling to see the cherry blossoms' beauty understood beauty much more. Enraptured by the beauty of the blossoms, they promptly danced in delight. This is real culture. Joy and delight are at the root of culture. Delight at seeing cherry blossoms during the flower viewing season forms part of the Japanese heritage, which is indispensable to Japanese culture.

I commented that, "Those at Hirosaki Castle must preserve its beautiful cherry blossom trees as well."

Hideo replied, "To preserve cherry-blossom trees is an expensive venture, so perhaps flower viewers should pay a fee. To maintain even a cultural building is costly and diverts funds from preserving the cherry-blossom trees."

Hideo had a size eight painting of cherry blossoms by Kigen Nakagawa in the sitting-room of the mountaintop house for some years. The name sounded something like *Harutōshi* (Far from Spring). It captured clumps of cherry-blossom trees in the foreground to the left, and below it a small stream flowing with a snow-capped mountain in the background, then layers of mountains behind it. The mountains appeared whitish grey, and the blossoms, soft and pale red, conveyed a sleepy mood.

Hideo explained this painting: "This is a painting of the noted, rare cherry blossoms at Takato, Ina, in Yamanashi prefecture. The blossoms were in full bloom when the Oda army attacked Takatō Castle, then shot and killed Nobumori Nishina, the younger brother of Katsuyori. His blood reputedly smeared the blossoms inside the castle, which thereafter were called 'blood-smeared cherry blossoms'."

I commented, "The blossoms in the painting do not seem very red; if smeared with blood, they should be a deeper red."

He said, "The blossoms are actually a much deeper red. A lovely colour. I went there twice and found them far from being a crude bloody red. They bloomed with a fascinating charm. People should care for them. Go to see them once. Go from Suwa city by car, although Suwa city also has some beautiful cherry blossoms. From Suwa, you cross the pass to Takatō. It is a fine town with good roads, having been a castle town in the past. The cherry blossoms bloom after 20 April, so I went once after checking the expected date of their full bloom, but I arrived a little late in 1962. Nakagawa had gone there, and painted the cherry blossoms. The furthest mountain is Mount Senjogatake of the Southern Alps."

I didn't ask him about the cherry blossoms in Suwa city, but I believe he meant those at Takashima Castle. Whenever talking about cherry blossoms, Hideo took delight. At night while drinking sake, he would talk on and on, "I saw the painting *Far from Spring* and praised it. When the dealer overheard me, he mistakenly reported to Nakagawa that I wanted to order it. Nakagawa thanked me by letter for the order, then sent me the painting."

Apparently, Hideo asked the dealer the price and went to Kigen Nakagawa's to deliver the money. Nakagawa, greatly pleased, brought out some whisky and provided a sumptuous meal, after which both became drunk in their joyful mood. Nakagawa fell asleep. As Hideo prepared to leave, he reached for the money, but it was gone. Alarmed, he searched about, worried that he had forgotten it, or had lost the money to a pickpocket. He did not have it. Hideo could not think well, his head spinning with the effect of the whisky. He had no recourse but to apologize to Nakagawa's grandson that he had somehow lost the money and would bring it another time. The grandson replied, "You already handed him the money." Nakagawa had put it in the drawer and the grandson took the sum from the drawer and showed it to Hideo. Greatly relieved, Hideo took his leave.

Afterwards, Nakagawa apologized for charging so much for the cherry-blossom painting, and painted for free an abstract portrait of Hideo, which he sent to him. It was this portrait that hung for so long in Hideo's study, and later was featured on the cover of the *Memorial Edition of Hideo Kobayashi* (Shinchōsha's Special Edition, April 1983).

Hideo's only daughter, Haruko, wrote a short essay, "His Last Viewing of Cherry Blossoms", for the cassette tape of her father's lecture "To Believe and to Know". For the first time, I read Haruko's writing, a well-written and moving piece.

It was ten days after the cherry-blossom viewing had begun at the end of March 1982 when my brother fell ill and was hospitalized. Apparently Hideo had persisted in seeing the drooping cherry blossoms at his Kamakura home and had convinced the head doctor to permit a weekend leave. In high spirits, he returned to Kamakura, but a typhoon-like storm the previous night had scattered most of the petals to the ground. When he arrived home he found the white petals blanketing the yard. The household expressed their disappointment and regret to Hideo that the storm had blown off most of the beautiful petals the previous day. But Hideo in great delight, nonetheless, looked at the flowerless tree as if possessed.

Returning to the hospital, Hideo repeatedly thanked the head doctor, who had enabled him to view these magnificent blossoms, which he thought he would not be able to see that year.

I read this in Haruko's essay, which brought tears to my eyes. I was deeply saddened, as I perceived both Hideo's sorrow and joy, and his relentless persistence.

Hideo himself used to say: "One truly sees when possessed by something. Only one possessed can be moved or awed. Those who are possessed are 'bewitched' or 'infatuated'."

However, this was reserved only for a person with superb sensitivity, capable of "seeing" or "being possessed". Hideo was capable of keen sensitivity, one who truly saw the cherry blossoms as if possessed.

Unable to transplant his cherry-blossom tree from the mountaintop house, Hideo had purchased another drooping cherry-blossom tree for his new prefab house. It too had beautiful blossoms, and Hideo impatiently waited for it to bloom every spring. One year, they bloomed so beautifully that he even invited the author Ton Satomi, then plagued with leg problems, to come and enjoy the flowers. It was this tree which Haruko had referred to in her essay.

Hideo's love for cherry blossoms turned fiendish, far beyond an ordinary interest. He became so obsessed that the blossoms could not but trigger in him a demonic passion for beauty.

At budding time, Hideo would always walk into the garden, stop below the tree, and gaze up at the branches, saying, "Can't they blossom sooner? I wonder when."

Also, during his study breaks, he would take out his binoculars and look at the buds from his second floor study. Once the blossoms appeared, he looked through the binoculars so often that the family in the house across the street closed the windows and drew the curtains to prevent Hideo from peeping into their bedroom. They probably thought Hideo was a peeping tom, but that was far-fetched. He was merely probing the beauty of the blossoms in deep appreciation. He had this childish innocence, and a fervour and passion that were inexplicable, I feel. I believe that few lovers of flowers and painters of beauty became so relentlessly attached to them as Hideo.

Chapter 20
A Person Who Searches His Intellect Alone Cannot Know His True Self

Hideo did not take to the theatre, although in his student days, he often saw kabuki plays. He once was moved to tears by Kikugorō Onoe VI's beautiful performance in "Dōjōji", and became engrossed for a period in Noh, but he never held an interest in modern drama. After World War II he briefly acted several times in the Literati Theatre at Bungei Shunjū's Bunshun Festival. He won acclaim for his role as the eldest son in Kan Kikuchi's drama *Father Returns* and prior to the war he performed in the Bungei Shunjū Readers' Meeting at Osaka around 1935, in his first performance ever in the Literati Theatre. He played the role of the barbarian in Takeo Arishima's *Domomata no Shi* (Death of Domomata), which I later saw in its Tokyo performance. Hideo humorously describes this in his free-style essay "Hatsu butai" (My First Performance; February 1936).

About that time I was invited to join the coterie magazine *Sakura* (Cherry Blossoms), published by such people as Taijirō Tamura, Tomoichirō Inoue, Takeo Kitahara and Ms Shizue Masugi, through which I became acquainted with Ms Masugi. At the urging of Ms Masugi, we decided to perform on stage Chekhov's *The Seagull*. It may have been a response to the Literati Theatre but Saneatsu Mushanokōji, who prior to this had a love affair with Shizue, became most enthusiastic and Ton directed the performance. The performers were recruited from former members of the then defunct Shingeki Research Centre headed by Kunio Kishida and Toyoo Iwata. Later Hana Nonaka, owner of the Ginza bar called Serenade, joined the cast under the name Mari Nonaka. Ms Masugi took the role of Masha, and I the role of Nina. We rented a rehearsal hall at Kagurazaka in Tokyo and rehearsed there almost daily. Satomi, as director, came almost every day, as did Mushanokōji, who apparently covered most of the expenses.

Hana Nakano published her book *Shōwa Kijin, Henjin, Omoshirojin* (Showa's Eccentrics, Lovers and Characters), but errs when she writes that Ms Shizue Masugi and I performed *The Seagull* after the war. The drama ran for about two days at Tsukiji Mini Theatre in 1936. Its props and settings were crude makeshifts, put together by backstage amateurs. Although the cast members concentrated on their performance, the rickety props and mismatched costumes concerned me far more than my acting.

I dared not suggest that Hideo come to such a play, but he did, perhaps through the urging or strong-arm tactics of Mushanokōji or Ton Satomi. He wrote about this in his free-style essay "Engeki ni Tsuite" (On Drama; October 1936).

> I've taken in few modern plays; but when I count them, most have been Chekhov's. Upon thinking back, the performances themselves have not been worth mentioning. Most recently, I saw *The Seagull*. The acting was amateurish, and the lines were spoken in various Japanese dialects ranging from northern Tōhoku to Southern Kyūshū, but these were not particularly disturbing. I felt that their successfully communicating Chekhov's spirit had overcome any defects in the performance. What had the performers accomplished? Of course, they had placed an accent on Chekhov's spirit, which I sense even when reading his works. That is, I have learned from modern drama a method by which to read works in print.
>
> I thought this in that theatre of modern plays, where I was a lone audience member.

This essay came as a relief, and revealed to me that drama could be viewed in such a light. I was grateful that he had not been disturbed by our faulty performance and lines that I thought deserved the severest of criticism. Of course, professional performers and, moreover, upcoming critics in the literary world would have judged Hideo's criticism as lacklustre or as an amateurish criticism of drama.

This essay, however, unveils Hideo's single-minded attitude regarding literature. He had not misconstrued the drama or acting but had understood only too well.

After the war, I wrote a drama called *Reikyūsha Totomoni* (With the Hearse), which was praised by Yutaka Mafune, then a playwright in Kamakura and a drinking friend of Hideo. He organized for it to be published in the theatre magazine *Engeki* (Drama). It was first performed by the Bungakuza Group, then later by two or three smaller theatrical groups, whose script Hideo read and commented on:

> It is written within safe limits. However, since all the characters are young and inexperienced, and very commonplace, the play seems to be not a drama but a show. It needs characters with impressive pasts and deep experiences to make it a solid drama. Ibsen's dramas give the smell of the past as soon as the curtain rises. Take the play *Ghost*. It

taunts the audience by hinting of incidents to come. The audience fears that a certain event will actually occur, towards which the audience is led in a natural way. Your play lacks this intensity, tension or pull. It lacks force—something which drama must have. This ingredient makes drama interesting. Next, your dialogues. Though they are interesting in their lightness and youthfulness, they lack genuine truth. A concrete truth must flow to make an appealing script. It is people with a rich experience and past that speak of this concrete truth.

This criticism hit me hard—but Hideo's criticism did not strike harshly in the way he demanded of his own writing, or as fiendishly as when he probed beauty. Rather, his criticism displayed a deep love for my work—this convincingly struck my heart. It drew me gradually to understand myself.

People assumed from Hideo's writings that he was too strict, frightening and complex for them to approach. Though wanting to meet Hideo, many feared to, particularly younger people. Having been involved with the YWCA since about 1935, some five girls aged about twenty begged me to take them to the hillside Ōgigayatsu house in 1938 to meet Hideo. These girls, graduates of middle schools and employed at companies and banks, admitted the difficulty of Hideo's writings. They initially appeared nervous, but began to ask some simple questions about the significance of humanism, the meaning of a syllogism and acquiring individuality. Hideo answered each question earnestly without belittling them.

He also gave his views regarding movies, then about novels:

> Movies in general are not good. We become imbeciles by watching them. They coerce us to either cry or laugh, so they are not pure. Novels, however, have great value in that each reader must use his head to imagine. Great novels develop imaginative powers. But novels today have little value. If I were the Minister of Education, I would ban all modern books and require the reading of classics. Once accustomed to reading good classics, one can immediately see the bad in books today. Readers today should read such works as those by Ashihei Hino.

Hideo also praised Shimei Futabatei's and Kunio Kishida's translations, then explained a way for people to find their potential in life.

> In ethics classes, schools instruct pupils to evaluate themselves, then repeatedly propagate the idea that mental self-evaluation results in self-understanding. But as long as one remains inactive, pupils never can understand themselves. Self-discovery only results from confronting actual problems and taking action about them. An inactive person, however, continues to evaluate himself and fails to understand himself.

He fails to apply himself physically. A person who searches his intellect alone cannot know his true self.

Hideo explained this so simply and patiently that the girls understood and were delighted. I was a little surprised that he answered so affectionately and diligently that ordinary girls could understand. They remarked how they had been stimulated and inspired.

About that time, two other unforgettable events occurred at the YWCA involving Hideo. The first involved Hideo consenting to speak at the YWCA after both the YWCA Secretary and I had asked him. The other involved my meeting the author Kanoko Okamoto through the YWCA. Both took place between autumn and winter of 1938.

The YWCA then—and perhaps today—used to enlist all its members for an annual autumn donation drive. A list of large companies and banks, and notable persons who were likely to donate was assigned each member, and they were asked to visit and ask for contributions for the education and welfare activities of the YWCA.

I disliked making visits to homes to solicit money, even for a good cause. I usually remained passive; but that year, I was instructed to see Kanoko. She had published numerous books in her uniquely flamboyant style, which flowed with burning passion. She had also written a series of articles in literary art magazines as well as women's magazines, which ranked her as a leading author in Japan. I had read her book *Seisei Ruten* (Vigorous Change) with great interest, and so I held her in high esteem.

Hideo also had recognized her unusual talents and, moreover, appreciated her financial help to keep in print *Bungakukai* magazine, which he edited.

I had seen her once at a concert with her husband, Ippei Okamoto, and was impressed by her large-framed body, thick black bobbed hair and large beautiful eyes. Ever since, I had wanted to meet and talk to her, then one day someone at the YWCA remarked to me, "Surely, she'll agree to meet the younger sister of Hideo Kobayashi."

So I telephoned her, and she kindly arranged an appropriate day to visit, giving me the directions to her home.

As I entered the old gate, I saw the large garden and the house with three doors set deep inside. Not knowing which door to approach, I pressed on the doorbell of the main entrance. An elderly woman appeared, asked my name, and went back inside. Soon the large-framed Kanoko with bobbed hair appeared and with a broad smile led me to the sitting-room.

After a simple greeting, she immediately inquired, "Is your brother well?"

The conversation concentrated on Hideo briefly, then at the first chance I spread some printed material before her somewhat anxiously, explained the donation drive and asked for a contribution. She listened intently, then nodded, stood up and left the room. Returning, she placed some money before me, saying, "Here you are."

I was relieved that all had proceeded so smoothly, and was very grateful that she was so willing to donate. I thought how splendid a person to contribute like this without asking any questions. So I bowed and then looked up, the amount of bills surprised me, all ten-yen bills, now probably each equivalent to over 20,000 yen. Not expecting half that amount, I excitedly put away the money, drew up a receipt and then resumed my talk with her.

Impressed by her energetic writings, which were being published in various literary sources every month, I asked how she maintained her vigour. She replied: "My mind is always filled with ideas for writing, and it remains full. So the pen moves smoothly. But, you know, I have so much to express, ideas appearing all at once, so that I have problems arranging them."

In deep admiration I listened, thinking how fortunate to be so gifted a person, compared to myself who was unable to write and express everything that came to my mind. I sat envying her talent.

Some moments passed, whereupon the elderly woman who had first met me at the door carried in wheat noodles on two lacquered wooden plates.

"These noodles prepared at a nearby shop are quite good. Please have some," Kanoko said, as she split her wooden disposable chopsticks. "I was scared, hearing over the phone that you were Hideo Kobayashi's younger sister. I am relieved now, to see how sweet you are and not fearsome like Hideo."

She said this while sucking up her noodles, and I felt sure that her remarks were not mere flattery. I could see that she meant every word. Coming from such a noted author, I felt honoured. Perhaps because of my elation, I thought the thin white noodles sprinkled on top with shredded seaweed and dipped in the soup all the more tasty.

Some days later, I visited the hillside Ōgigayatsu house and told Kiyomi about Kanoko Okamoto. Kiyomi explained that Kanoko had once confessed in tears to Hideo that she loved him deeply. This was so like Kanoko, I thought, remembering her kindness that day and the delicious noodles she had served me. I had envied her good fortune, but then felt the misfortune and sadness that author had actually faced in real life.

I wondered how Hideo, then aged thirty-six—who himself had ten years before suffered from his love for Yasuko—would have reacted to a woman thirteen years his senior confessing her love for him. I had no idea, but I felt that Kanoko had been expressing in her writings her frustrated and unfulfilled love all along.

Four months after I had visited her home, she suddenly passed away in February 1939. In great dismay, I went to pay my condolences on the first

Seventh Day Memorial, where her husband, Ippei Okamoto, and the author Nobuko Yoshiya sat with red, tearful eyes.

Kanoko had reportedly died of brain haemorrhage, but later I heard it was suicide. I didn't know the truth nor did I care to know. However, if it was suicide, it seemed strange that a woman of such will power could not overcome her distress and discover the sacredness of life. Hideo had twice considered suicide in his twenties, but had reconfirmed that life was sacred and not his to take. Whatever the cause of Kanoko's death, it was a great tragedy to prematurely lose this talented author still in her late fifties.

Chapter 21
I Do Things Out Of Personal Obligation Only

Each time a book of Hideo's was published Kiyomi unfailingly kept one for me, so I have received most of them. They fill one section of my bookcases, the other shelves contain inferior, insignificant books. I am grateful for having received so many of his books.

Aside from his books, I have received too little else from Hideo, except for some half-dozen gifts.

His first gift to me was a copy of Shinran's *Tannishō*, which he sent me from Kyoto during his vagabond year. The second gift was a bottle of perfume, which he purchased for me in the Ginza the following year when his essay "Various Patterns" had been placed second in the *Kaizō* magazine contest. He bought me mainly souvenirs. He bought me a greenish jade sash-clip during his trip to Korea, Manchuria and Northern China at the end of 1938. Then, after his extended travels in Europe with Hidemi Kon in 1953, he gave me two brooches bought in Paris, a leather purse and an ancient Grecian coin. Hideo had selected the two uniquely designed brooches with the help of Fubuki Koshiji, who was then in Paris—I still have one. The crimson purse is of high quality leather; I used it with care, but thirty years' of wear and tear have made it impractical for use in public, though the cochineal leather itself remains unmarked and lustrous.

Hideo explained the Grecian coin to me: "Though many fakes are sold in Greece, I bought it at a shop where a person I trusted claimed only authentic articles were sold. Upon my return to Japan, I asked Mizuno, a Greek scholar, to show me a genuine piece, and I realized that the coin was a near-perfect replica of the genuine. It was a fake after all, six or seven of these fakes had cost a total of 150 dollars, the price of one genuine coin."

I appreciated Hideo telling me this. However, when I showed it to Takamizawa, he wanted it for himself. I had to forgo making a pendant with it. When I explained this to Hideo, he became angry, "Don't ever give away a gift that I give you!"

I tilted my head to one side, perplexed. Later I realized that Hideo chose his gifts with great care and sincerity.

The next gift was in exchange for my bed that Haruko wanted when she was fourteen or fifteen. I wanted for it a small, old Chinese perfume container of original colour, three centimetres in diameter that Hideo had once shown me. He agreed only reluctantly. It was an odd trade, my enormous bed for a small perfume container, which turned out to be the most priceless among the things I had received from Hideo. I still display it in my room.

I received another gift later in the mid-1950s. I had met Hideo quite by chance at Ginza Station, on the platform of the Marunouchi subway line.

"I dislike subways," he said. "I can't find my way out and always take the wrong exit." Hideo started to walk, leading me out almost at random. The exits were not clearly marked in those days so, although obvious to someone who was careful to find the right exit, I often took the wrong one and became confused. Anyway, we both somehow made it out to Ginza Street.

"Let's have something to drink," he said.

We were having coffee at the Shiseidō Coffee Shop, when Hideo said, "I want to buy Haruko a good handkerchief. Please help me, I'll buy you one too."

Unfamiliar with handkerchief embroideries and not knowing Haruko's tastes, I was somewhat at a loss, but finally Hideo and I selected one. He bought one for me as well. This, of course, after so many years I have misplaced, but even such a small thoughtfulness reminds me of his affection.

Hideo was a true Japanese at heart; he enthusiastically read Japanese history, loved the literary classics and deeply respected Japan's past and traditions.

About ten years ago, the publication of Isaiah Ben Dasan's bestseller *Nihonjin to Yudayajin* (The Japanese and the Jews; 1975) sparked a flood of studies and publications that compared Japanese traits to one thing or another. Hideo sharply disagreed with such views about unique or typical characteristics of the Japanese. In general, it was thought that the modern Japanese differed considerably from the Japanese of the ancient Manyō days. The assumption was made that Japan's lengthy history, culture and political system had coloured, influenced, distorted and altered Japanese traits but Hideo preferred to believe that we were not so different from primitive Japanese.

The Japanese are said to value affection and obligations, to know shame and to observe numerous ceremonies and formalities. The Japanese hold endless celebrations and commemorations, such as those of the year-end, homecomings and farewells, book launches, and special sixtieth and seventieth birthday parties. Hideo hated these, refusing invitations from even the Emperor's Household and the Prime Minister, which most Japanese would feel duty-bound to accept.

Also, Hideo usually disdained the practice of giving year-end gifts, New Year's cards, souvenirs and visiting gifts, a custom the Japanese observe for formality's sake.

The Japanese have long held to obligations that, emptied of true feeling today, have become a mere face-saving device. The prevalence of the phrase "perfunctory obligation" indicates this trend. Of course, the Japanese resort to this to win the respect of others and to retain their good standing, a practice Hideo hated. Instead, Hideo spoke his mind, though this was often misunderstood and costly to him.

Feudalistic ways still remain. Japanese discriminate between people even in "democratic" Japan today, as seen in the language. Many use honorifics to address people of higher status, reputation and ability, and vulgar language to address equals or those of lower status. Out of courtesy, Hideo initially greeted everyone politely, but his language then turned vulgar, regardless of the person's status. He once met prime ministers Yoshida and Satō, and addressed them in vulgar idiomatic Japanese. He showed no inclination to impress them.

In Hideo's university years, his irresponsible life inevitably caused problems, which required favours from others. However, he never forgot his deep indebtedness to them. Among them was Professor Tatsuno, Hideo's mentor at university. The penniless Hideo had received shoes and other items from this professor. He also opened his personal library to Hideo, enabling him to read freely many books unavailable then. Hideo brought his personal concerns to him as well. Although unable to repay his indebtedness, Hideo well understood Professor Tatsuno's magnanimity as a person. Having his prize-winning essay "Various Patterns" published in the reputable *Kaizō* magazine in 1929 only a year after graduating from university, Hideo wrote a criticism of Professor Tatsuno's book two years later. He writes thus:

> Professor Tatsuno was my mentor at university. He was no pushover. As a wayward student, I had caused my mentor an endless amount of trouble for which I still feel indebted to him. From a mentor's viewpoint, he probably found me impossible. Anyway, any fellow who knew me would say that I was considered far worse than undeserving. Those who know me might be reading this essay. So I feel I should say to those that to comment on Professor Tatsuno's book is a formidable task for me. I have to admit that the very fact that I was a wayward student had drawn upon me the professor's kindness and affection. You exemplary students, may I ask you to consider my predicament?

As a teacher too, Professor Tatsuno apparently excelled. During Hideo's trying and irresponsible university days, I feel that only God's grace and good fortune had brought Hideo and Professor Tatsuno together. Hideo, too, undeniably felt so.

Some ten years later, Hideo made sure to attend Professor Tatsuno's final lecture upon his retirement from Tokyo Imperial University. Hideo gave greetings on behalf of the graduates of the French Literature Department. In his remarks, Hideo said, "Socrates said, a good teacher enables his students to discover themselves."

I believe that thanks to this teacher, Hideo had literally discovered himself. Although Hideo disliked attending matters not in his heart, or problems regarding human ties, he complied with the requests of those he felt indebted to from the past.

The year 1938 was a hectic one for Hideo. He was sent to China in March of that year as a special correspondent for *Bungei Shunjū* magazine and as a courier of the Akutagawa Award to Ashihei Hino. He returned a month later at the end of April, quite tanned and holding two large suitcases. The whole Kamakura literati group came to meet him and held a festive drinking party that night at the Kafūen Inn in Kamakura. My husband and I were also invited and stayed overnight at the inn. He left once again that year in October, this time for Manchuria, Harbin and Peking, and returned in December. He was fatigued, but agreed to lecture that month at the YWCA, out of a genuine desire to make good my request. He said more or less the following:

> Fiction fails to depict life since life cannot be adequately expressed by novels. Authors merely interpret life in novels. Flaubert merely interpreted life, and Hoffman wrote that life bordered on insanity more than depicted in novels. Poe too understood the abyss of life, which he expressed in his eerie novels....
>
> The notions of Bushidō and the Yamato spirit are not pre-eminent, but the Japanese people themselves are. To assert a return to the past is wrong. We must import more of Western culture. Within our polite formalities, we must learn how to bring out our individuality.

The tone in the latter half was unlike Hideo. During the Sino–Japanese War he was probably angered by the shallowness of the Japanese people who had been swept along by the haughtiness of the Japan National and Pure Japan Nationalism movements.

Hideo often said to me, "Value your friendships, because you alone are responsible for selecting and developing them. Those reared in the same generation can understand each other. Your children are born and reared in a different generation, so gaps arise. You should value your friends."

Hideo cared for his friends. Or perhaps, he respected them. Of course, he felt affection for and "obligated" toward those through whom he had learned much. Despite his reservations, he often agreed to their requests.

During the war, around 1943, Hideo lectured on the "Bungakusha no Teikei ni Tsuite" (Joint Effort of Writers) at the Wartime Conference of Writers of the Greater Asia Co-Prosperity Sphere. On this occasion too, Hideo had only agreed to lecture because Tetsutarō Kawakami served on the committee for the conference.

Hideo later told Kawakami, "I spoke because you, a friend, had requested it; otherwise I would have declined."

At a time when writers joined in eagerly to cooperate with the Co-Prosperity Movement, Hideo spoke in a way to dash it to pieces. Nonetheless, what he said rang true. He concluded with:

> Of course this great joint effort requires the cooperation of politicians, their political means and organizations. However, the real harmony of writers, in short, comes from the joy of creative writing, often not understood by people, or from understanding each other's difficulties. I believe joining hands is as difficult as fighting a war.

Around the time Hideo was moving to the Swedish prefab house near the Hachiman Shrine (in January 1976), Hideo and Hidemi Kon conducted a dialogue at the Mainichi Newspaper Office. He says in this dialogue:

> I really didn't feel up to coming here. I am unable [in spoken words] to say anything worthy. You [Hidemi Kon] asked me to, so I came through my obligation to a lifelong friend. I do things only out of personal obligations. This is the spirit of a man of literature, I believe.

In this respect, Hideo liked the ways of the Japanese people. As a true Japanese, however, his practice of "human affection and obligation" (*giri-ninjō*) contrasted sharply with what was customary.

He almost never visited relatives. Whenever I visited him, however, he welcomed me, providing sumptuous meals while talking on simple topics. He inquired about family members. Also, with others he talked mainly on common topics easy to converse on, such as their life and work.

However, he rarely visited relatives' homes. He did once take the trouble to visit our house at the time we lived next door to Kōshirō Onchi in Ogikubo in Tokyo, whose house had been designed by Arata Endō. So our house would fit in, we too had our house designed by Arata Endō and painted it the same dark brown colour. This was in 1940 when we could capture a view of the Chichibu Mountains and Mount Fuji from the second floor. This is where my mother often visited us with Kiyomi, but Hideo never did. Whenever I went to Kamakura, I invited Hideo to visit; Kiyomi too encouraged him to visit us. Hideo would agree and ask for directions, but he never came.

It was around 1 a.m. when the doorbell suddenly rang, waking Takamizawa and me. Surprised and somewhat frightened because it was so late at night, I inquired, "Who is it?" before opening the front door.

"It's me, Hideo," he said in his usual high-pitched voice. He had surprised me again. Coming for the first time and in the dark, he had apparently searched round and round in a taxi. However, once in the area, he boasted that he had found the house by instinct. My husband woke up and came downstairs, then drank a while with Hideo. I put out some side dishes, but since it was late, Hideo soon went to bed. The next day, after a late breakfast, he returned to Kamakura.

Whenever I asked him, he usually came to places other than our home. He disliked publicizing the works of others, but around 1967 at the publication of the *Norakuro Zenshū* (Complete Norakuro), Hideo came after an editor of a weekly magazine had me request his presence. He came all the way from Kamakura. At the department store, he talked with Takamizawa and agreed to have photographs taken together.

Also, on a previous occasion around 1959 when Kōdansha Publishers held a reception at the Chinzansō Gardens, Hideo appeared and invited us to a meal. "Let's go have some sushi," he said, leading us to a delicious sushi restaurant.

Hideo said, "I received some money for writing the article on *Norakuro* for the *Bungei Shunjū* magazine, so I'll treat you both."

This eventually became the essay "Cartoon" (1959), later included in his book *Kangaeru Hinto* (Hints for Thought).

Chapter 22
Be Thankful For Something Cherished, Then Relinquish It

Uncle Moku and Aunt Wakana Jōya, who had always helped us, passed away in Kamakura. This left only Uncle Saburō, who was reared with us in the same house, and his wife, Yūko. They both supported us in a personal way. Of course, Hideo had not visited Uncle Saburō's house, but often sent gifts and notable souvenirs from places he visited in Japan.

In February 1977, at Keiō Hospital, Uncle Saburō eventually died at the age of eighty-three. He had spent his last year or two in and out of the hospital. Hideo had visited him there. When the doctor told him that Uncle Saburō had but a week left, Hideo visited him twice that week, firmly clasping his hands to express his deep sorrow.

After the funeral, relatives and friends placed flowers in the coffin, but Hideo stood motionless at the foot of the coffin throughout the service. He then placed his flower last, and stood there alone after the coffin had been closed, carried away, and the mourners had filed outside.

Before going to the crematorium, Hideo, as the family representative, was asked to address the mourners lined along the road to see the hearse off. Asked on the spot to speak, Hideo was at a loss, but began to stammer along. Usually Japanese open their remarks with "For troubling yourselves to attend this service..." to thank the mourners, but Hideo omitted this and immediately began talking about Uncle Saburō.

> Uncle Saburō carried on my father's work and devoted his lifetime to it. He was a creative craftsman. He put his heart in perfecting diamonds, without publicizing or writing about them. He was a craftsman who earnestly sought that satisfaction and joy when parting from his perfected work, and then continued to create. Only recently have I understood this noble task of the craftsman. I am writing something now, which I had wanted Uncle Saburō to read; but unfortunately....

That year, in October, his series "Motoori Norinaga", which had appeared in *Shinchō* magazine, was published as a book. Hideo was probably referring to this. Hideo refuted those aesthetes who in their aesthetic studies placed trust in creativity but belittled craftsmanship. Hideo liked craftsmen who quietly created day after day, purely for the sake of the work, with no other thought in mind.

"I too am a kind of craftsman," Hideo used to say. He loved the paintings by Georges Roualt (1871–1958), the son of a cabinet-maker who became a stained-glass artisan in his youth and began painting after entering art school at the age of twenty. He had spent his life following the spirit of craftsmanship, patiently applying himself body and soul.

In the process of addressing the mourners, Hideo suddenly changed his tone, as if speaking directly to Uncle Saburō himself.

"Our Mammy, our Mammy...."

Since our childhood days, Hideo and I had called our mother *Okka-san* (Mammy). This was because Hideo had been born in uptown Sarugaku in Kanda, and I in Nandomachi in Ushigome in Shinjuku ward, later moving to Shirokane, a wealthy area in Shiba, Tokyo. Consequently, though I was reared in the upper class Yamanote area, I grew up hearing the uptown term "Mammy" used by Hideo. Those days the upper class Yamanote homes used the words "Mama", "Mother" or "Mom"; never the word "Mammy". As I entered fifth grade in primary school, I remember my embarrassment when I realized the crudeness of this word. At home, however, the word "Mammy" prevailed, even with Uncle Saburō, who used it in referring to our mother. Among Uncle Saburō and Hideo and I, "Mammy" sounded most natural and intimate.

In adulthood, Hideo began using words such as "my old woman" or "Mom" when talking to others about her. So some years had elapsed since he last used the word "Mammy". Hideo had much to say, not to the mourners before him but to Uncle Saburō, using expressions most natural between them. I felt the pureness of Hideo's affection for Saburō, his feelings of indebtedness to him.

The Japanese are diligent, productive, efficient and sensitive to others because they are concerned for their own image, but Hideo appeared relaxed whenever I visited in the evenings. Perhaps he had so mentally taxed himself in writing that after working hours he enjoyed himself fully, appearing anything but diligent and efficient.

The Japanese are not only ambiguous and sensitive to other's reactions but also use meaningless flattery and lip service, which Hideo abhorred. Seeing this in others angered him. He made certain he spoke only the truth regardless of the enmity it brought him. People, in fact, disliked and misunderstood him.

Hideo's generation, born in the Meiji Period, cherished their past and their birthplace, viewing things in an irrational, nostalgic way. This probably stems from ancestor worship, although the younger generation no longer holds to it.

Hideo valued Japanese history and the past as well. He warned against grasping at the new at the price of losing Japanese sensitivity towards nature and a respect for the past. He sought a human spirituality in them, not something arising from customs and formalities. He had toast and coffee in the small dining room adjoining the kitchen at the hillside Ōgigayatsu house. When Hideo started to play golf in the 1950s, he began wearing Western clothes even at home and slept on a bed, and added a Western-style study and sitting-room at the mountaintop house. After breakfast, he would scatter three newspapers on the sitting-room sofa to read, and practised putting before entering his study to work. At times, he studied in the sitting-room, as his mood dictated that day. For lunch he went from the mountaintop to a noodle shop near Kamakura Station, taking a walk along the way. He did little work in the afternoon, and never from evening onwards. In the summer, after taking a quick bath, he changed into a bathrobe and in the winter, into a wool kimono, then enjoyed his leisurely evening drinking sake in the straw-mat room. In this respect, he was a true Japanese.

Hideo loved young soya beans—the small kind not yet fully grown. These were boiled in salt water and poured into a deep dish, which he would offer to me but finish off by himself. In his later years, a little after supper he would ask for a pillow and lay spread out in the straw-mat room. Initially, his prefab house at Yukinoshita was completely done in the Western style but, wanting a place to recline, he had added a Japanese-style room where he relaxed in the evening until bedtime.

At present every room in that house has a photo of Hideo. However, in his favourite Japanese-style room an old miniature five-storey pagoda and the emerald green comma-shaped bead that Hideo always carried in his pocket to feel with his fingers are placed in front of his photo. Also, Hideo's favourite seasonal flowers—cherry blossoms, camellias, bellflowers, chrysanthemums, and wild pinks—are placed there. On the wall above the photo are hung Dogyū Okumura's original painting of some wild cherry blossoms, which appears on the fly page of *Motoori Norinaga*, and a scroll originally painted by Motoori Norinaga himself.

After he had moved down from the mountaintop house in 1976, leaving his home of almost thirty years, I looked back at the last ten years. I was impressed how completely he had severed himself from the home of his past without any qualms.

Near the end of his essay "Mozart", he mentions that he never complained when having to settle for something less because he had lacked the time to set goals, to devise the approach and to concentrate. He follows with:

> The following is perhaps incomprehensible for a complainer: a complainer is incompatible with himself. He blames the incompatibility on other people and his environment, thinking it is a matter of "struggling against and overcoming his environment". Beethoven struggled against himself and was victorious. In other words, a person of strong will power accepts an adverse environment as it is, as lacking nothing. It desires to struggle only against this genuine foe, not against a benign foe. The capacity for life enables one to see that exterior, spontaneous occurrences are matters for the inner self to deal with. This is a religious idea, but not an empty one. Great complainers called social reformers find this idea incomprehensible. They have never realized that the source of man's happiness or unhappiness is within.

People blame an adverse environment on other people and on a society they think they must overcome. Their environment is actually an inevitable factor that they must accept. They fail to realize that true victory comes by winning a struggle within oneself.

He also said, "It is a mistake to cling to what we cherish, to regret parting from it. When the time comes, we must part with it, thankful for having enjoyed it."

This also meant to look forward to a new environment when the change occurs. We must abandon the past, graciously retaining it as beautiful reminiscences and then look forward.

Hideo's strength of will enabled him to pursue new matters to their limits, including his capability to accept any change of environment.

The mountaintop house was located in a truly quiet and relaxing area, surrounded by nature's richness and a spectacular view without a housetop in sight. But his prefab house was surrounded by houses on all sides without a view even from upstairs. The house was around half the size of the yard at the mountaintop house; the yard was too small for practising putting.

Still, Hideo eagerly found new tasks here hitherto not possible at the mountaintop house and threw himself into them. He began to take daily walks in the morning. Even in the winter, he woke first and, going out about 6:30, he walked for over an hour through the nearby Hachiman Shrine precincts to Daitō Shrine and returned to have breakfast.

He seemed so enthusiastic and would say, "Kamakura still has its old, quiet back streets, which I take pleasure in."

Next, he devoted himself to landscape gardening—a new undertaking perhaps not possible until then. He had moved to the prefab house at the age of seventy-four. Counting on ten more good years, he planned his garden accordingly. To view flowers as soon as possible, he looked for trees that would blossom within a short time.

First, he had his favourite cherry-blossom tree planted in the centre of the yard. It was a manly and sturdy tree of twenty years, and purported to be a double-blossom tree. However, it managed to bloom only single-blossom flowers. Nonetheless, the magnificent beauty of the blossoms fully satisfied Hideo. Next he had a wild cherry-blossom tree planted beside the front gate, and then a Japanese Romeda tree. Then, for the first time ever, he started to visit nurseries, searching for trees to his taste. Beside the cherry-blossom tree, he had a plum tree planted. Then he bought several varieties of camellias, which made the yard look like a garden.

Books like *Planning and Designing Gardens* and *Garden Patches*, which had not previously interested him, lay on his desk—he repeatedly read these, absorbing himself in garden design. On early morning walks, he would enter someone else's garden, though the house's occupants happened to be asleep, and stroll around for a closer look. Finding a good garden, he either took a leisurely look until he was contented or carefully studied it.

Under the cherry-blossom tree, he placed a bluish *tsukuba* slate stone of handsome shape. Absorbing himself in rocks, he had gone around in search for them. This particular one he had found in a nursery in Totsuka near Yokohama while he was plant hunting. A stepping-stone there caught his fancy and, after a long look, he asked: "Won't you sell me this stepping stone?"

"There's nothing we won't sell," the man answered.

Overjoyed, Hideo had the stone dug up and delivered to his home.

Hideo was not easy to satisfy because of his persistence, but then nor were Mozart or Musashi Miyamoto. However Hideo adhered to the belief that life continued on, and he never complained about his new circumstances —always finding new tasks to do because of his resilience.

Chapter 23
I Am Prone To Injury

From our childhood, Hideo and I differed vastly. In our youth, at the Shirokane house, we had two gramophones. One was a common household type with a big horn shaped like a morning glory and a handle. The other was the older cylinder type. A cylinder-record was attached and the cock wound, which revolved the cylinder and moved the aluminium horn with a "sound box" at the end to produce the sound.

Father had purchased the latter in America around the time of the Russo–Japanese War, and although it is a collector's item today no one in the household then took any interest in it. Only Hideo, then in primary school, used to bring it out and listen to it. Each cylinder was kept in a firm, round canister. We had six. I had from first grade begun *koto* lessons of the Yamada-school style, and from third grade traditional *nagauta* ballad lessons—so I lacked the keen sensitivity for appreciating Western music, though I was interested in it.

Hideo's interests differed from mine, as he made this gramophone his favourite plaything in his primary school days. He particularly liked one of the six cylinder-recordings, a melancholy sounding one that he listened to repeatedly without knowing the title. Later, in his days in Kansai, he was deeply moved when he identified the music he had been listening to as Mozart's *Fagotto Concerto*.

Having repeatedly listened to Mozart's music in vague appreciation as a child, by adulthood Hideo enjoyed classical music by many composers. He studied not only the works of Mozart but also those of Bach and Beethoven. He became so engrossed in stereo music that Yasusuke Gomi's replies to his innumerable questions enabled Hideo to construct a good quality stereo set. For this achievement, the music critic Hidekazu Yoshida described Hideo as "a man drunk on music".

Risaburō Sasabe, Hideo's childhood friend of the same age, graduated from Shirokane Primary School and entered First Middle School with him. Around the sixth grade, Mr Ozawa had brought him and other pupils to our house to hear our father talk about his foreign travels, then later had a photograph taken with Sasabe sitting next to Hideo, as one of the seven in the class to enter First Middle School. After graduating from First Middle School, Sasabe entered the Naval Academy and served in the marines in Shanghai during Hideo's university days, then finally became a marine captain in the Pacific War. Being on good terms, since his house was nearby, Hideo and Sasabe often exchanged visits. Of the times I met him I was most impressed, perhaps, in the summer of my fifth year in girls' middle school when he visited the Shirokane house wearing a white Naval Academy uniform and a white cap with gold stars. In contrast to his middle school days, he had transformed himself into a dashing young man. As he prepared to leave, I bowed and bade him farewell. He lifted his right hand to his cap and saluted me with a quick smile. Saluted for the first time, I blushed, my heart pounding excitedly.

I read an article about ten years ago where Daizō Kusayanagi interviewed Mr Sasabe about Hideo. Apparently, in his First Middle School days Hideo excelled in English and Japanese but not in mathematics. However, in those days Hideo was good enough to help me to understand applied mathematics, explaining it by drawing numerous diagrams on paper, then later algebra and geometry once I entered girls' middle school. Although he did not excel in mathematics, he was capable enough to teach me. Sasabe also describes Hideo as honest, direct, quiet and good-looking, so that Sasabe's mother always referred to Hideo as the pretty boy.

In the summer of our primary school days, we went to Tadoshima Island in Ago Bay in Shima, Mie prefecture, known for its Mikimoto cultured pearls. There, Hideo bought for Sasabe a baby sea horse bottled in alcohol, a noted souvenir of that area. Sasabe says he still has it.

In his second year at First Higher School, Hideo's novella *Suicide of the Octopus* was published in the coterie magazine *Kyōon*, and later praised by Naoya Shiga. Hideo brought Sasabe a copy, saying, "This is my first novella in print. One of the characters is modelled after you, so here's a copy." This startled Sasabe.

The reason is, throughout First Middle School Hideo had not participated in the coterie magazine put out by many classmates, but suddenly, after entering First Higher School, he wrote a novella. Sasabe believes that our father's sudden death, the family's financial problems, our mother's illness and his own nervous condition, all occurring in 1921, had prompted it.

Mr Ozawa, Hideo's primary-school class teacher, had long recognized Hideo's writing skills, and had even given Hideo a pen-name. So I believe Hideo had desired to write since his middle-school days. Moreover, his middle-school classmates included such future writers as Jōji Ishimaru and Shōzaburō Kimura and, one year above him, his close companions were Tarō Tominaga, Korehito Kurahara and Tetsutarō Kawakami. Having such friends,

Hideo undoubtedly aspired to write. He read literature voraciously. In middle school, Jun'ichirō Tanizaki's *Grief of a Mermaid* had so impressed him that his re-readings had enabled him to memorize it. Among others, he had read most of the works of Dostoevsky, Tolstoy, Turgenev and Maupassant. However, he did not actually write creatively until higher school, which most likely was provoked by the burdens Hideo bore, as Sasabe has explained above.

The writer Masuji Ibuse explains: "All four—Hideo Kobayashi, Kenzō Nakajima, Tetsutarō Kawakami and Ibuse himself" had been "reared by mothers alone, since [their] fathers died early". Without a father to depend on and support them, those "reared by mothers alone" develop a relentless will for life from a young age. Youthful energy normally exerted to assert independence from a father is turned inwards into self-struggle, resulting in a pitiful battle with the self.

This reminds me of Hideo, who also turned violent whenever in a period self-struggle.

During the time Sasabe was stationed in Shanghai as a commissioned marine, Hideo visited Sasabe's house with Sakiko. Around 1927, Sakiko's illness had turned critical, forcing them to move four or five times before settling in Shirokane-dai. Living near Sasabe's house had provoked nostalgic childhood memories. Hideo surprised Sasabe's mother, who found Hideo poverty stricken in his worn-out clothing and vastly changed in demeanour since primary-school days. She wrote to Sasabe that the pretty boy had come, bringing a street girl with him. Here again we can see Hideo's brash innocence at work, or perhaps his fearless straightforwardness.

Hideo remembered Shirokane as the nostalgic home of his primary and middle-school days. Returning to this place after three years, he probably visited Sasabe's house, hoping to meet his childhood friend. Without second thoughts he had taken Sakiko, whose looks and manners resembled a street girl.

Though stricken by Sakiko's illness and lack of money, this period constituted some of his proudest days. He refused to bow for favours to write articles for money. Rather, at a Kamakura beach he met an editor from *Bungei Shunjū* who asked Hideo to write articles after seeing the life Hideo lived. Hideo wrote these anonymously. Also, he tutored French to Shōhei Ōoka and Tetsutarō Kawakami, boasting: "I'll do you the favour of teaching you French, so ask me to be your tutor." He was in financial need, which, however, never depressed him in the least. He would rent a house, make it dirty, leave it in a mess to his heart's content, then declare haughtily, "Such a dirty place is unfit for me."

Houses for rent were plentiful in those days, enabling both him and Sakiko to take this attitude.

Hideo left Sakiko in May 1928. I am unsure of the details of Sakiko's life. However, I heard that in December the same year she returned to live with Nakahara, then left Nakahara for another fellow the following year and had a child.

Hideo had returned to Tokyo from Kansai the year before and lived with us for two years without mentioning Sakiko to me. Sakiko, however, writes in her articles that she greeted him when she met him, but they never really conversed. I too had occasionally chanced upon Sakiko, but we parted without talking much about her activities. In 1955, I was serving as receptionist for the Tokyo YWCA's Fiftieth Anniversary Commemoration during its exhibition "Health and Women's Life" in Nihonbashi's Mitsukoshi Department Store, when Sakiko showed up. She told me she had become a believer of "Ohikari-sama" (Teaching of Salvation) and was active in its work.

Sakiko recounted that she occasionally visited Hideo in Kamakura. Hideo, living then at the mountaintop house, apparently brought out a tea bowl and asked her to buy it, which she did for a hundred yen. Although Hideo might have been in financial difficulty when he lived alone with my mother in Kamakura, his economic situation had improved by the time he moved to the mountaintop house after the war, so he had no need to sell a tea bowl for money. Also, selling a tea bowl for a hundred yen after the war sounds far too cheap. Moreover, Kiyomi claims that Hideo refused to see Sakiko when she occasionally visited the mountaintop house. It was Kiyomi who received her and provided meals when mealtime approached. Hideo never came out.

On one occasion, Hideo had gone to Itō in Izu Peninsula or somewhere when she visited his house. She asked his whereabouts and went to Itō by taxi. Evidently, Hideo told her to return, and paid the taxi fare. Pained deeply by the unnerving nightmarish past with her, Hideo undoubtedly found unbearable the thought of seeing her again. Any normal man would have found it unbearable. It is incomprehensible to me how Sakiko could visit Hideo in Kamakura forgetting their agonizing years as if they never happened.

After Hideo's death, Sakiko reminisced about those days, laughing, "At first his wife resented my visits, but then she got used to them."

Since Hideo took care of himself from his fifties and sixties on, he stayed healthy, but his life before then had been reckless and often left him ill. He once approached death, then was often hospitalized even after his marriage. In 1938, he came down with ulcers; then in 1942, during the war, he was hospitalized in a hospital in Hibiya specializing in stomach and intestine diseases, again for ulcers. Since no white rice was available—only a handful of rationed hard black rice—during the wartime scarcity I remember bringing some white rice provided by a former pupil of mine in Saitama prefecture. Whenever I visited him in hospital, I went with some nourishing rice gruel for him. Then in 1952, just before mother's Seventh Memorial Service, Hideo came down with pneumonia. His condition had improved, but as a precaution he did not attend the service. Work had prevented my husband Takamizawa too from attending, so only Kiyomi and I went to the temple in Aoyama, Tokyo, and had the sutra read. On the way home, we lunched at Ume-Chaya Restaurant—in the back streets of the Ginza where Hideo often drank those days—where we had their delicious fried trout.

Not only was he often ill, he also incurred serious injuries on numerous occasions. He himself described this tendency thus: "I am prone to injury." On a ski trip, he seriously injured his thigh; fractured his collarbone when he fell while getting off a ski lift; and fractured his ribs and lost consciousness when he fell off the platform at Suidōbashi Station. Moreover twice in his twenties he considered suicide but reconsidered, and, later, he barely escaped being killed.

As Sakiko's illness grew worse, she came close to killing Hideo several times. Then, from the Sino-Japanese War through the tribulations of World War II, he narrowly escaped death twice in Nanking in 1943, and once prior to that in Shanghai in 1938. The first time, Hideo ran into Torao Saitō, a former First Middle School classmate, in Shanghai as he returned after delivering, as a special correspondent of *Bungei Shunjū*, the Akutagawa Prize to Ashihei Hino who was then in China. Saitō had been assigned to Shanghai as a special airforce attaché reporter by *Asahi Newspaper*. The two became dead drunk after emptying five bottles of John Haig originally purchased by Saito as gifts to take back to Japan. The next morning, Hideo put on Saitō's worn-out attaché uniform, put the *Bungei Shunjū* band around the sleeve and left. But he fell into an opposition party's ploy that ordered him to be shot. In the nick of time, Yukio Iwata came to his rescue.

The second occasion, which Daizō Kusayanagi writes about, occurred in December 1943 in Nanking, where Hideo had gone for the Greater Far East Co-Prosperity Literati Meeting. The Information Bureau had originally planned it for Tokyo, but when Chairman Masao Kume insisted on Nanking, the bureau had conceded. Thus, the literati group pushed for the meeting in Nanking through the Kodama Organization. Hideo went with them, but while drinking with the Kodama Organization members he got involved in an argument, raining down criticisms on the bossy Hikotarō Yoshida. Yoshida, in a fury later forced his way into the inn with the intention of cutting off Hideo's arm. Hideo was sleeping so peacefully, like a Buddha, that Yoshida dropped the idea and left.

The other occurrence took place on a train, when Hideo got drunk while drinking with Lin Pai-sheng and began patting his head. The M.P. officers mistakenly assumed Hideo was striking the official's head and gave the order, "Do away with that Kobayashi." Overhearing this order, Jūkichi Kō gen, who admired Hideo for criticizing Hikotarō Yoshida, approached the M.P. officers and put in a good word, "Kobayashi is a fellow indispensable to Japan. Don't do anything to him."

Thanks to him, so the story goes, Hideo managed to escape with his life.

Whenever Hideo drank, his sharp tongue lashed out regardless of whom it was, insulting and angering them; but Hideo's words rang with truth and hit the mark, which gained the admiration of even the likes of Jūkichi Kōgen. What others held back in fear of reprisal, Hideo spoke out unafraid. When Hideo was drinking with Masao Kume—the leader of Japan's wartime literary world, and his senior—Kume once muttered, "I won't be able to write, I'm drinking so much. In tomorrow's series, I will perhaps add a lot of dialogues to intentionally give it length."

"So you call yourself a writer, do you?" Hideo evidently retorted, denouncing this writer's slack attitude toward his own writing.

Having moved to the mountaintop house in the scarcity of the postwar era, Hideo had many things stolen. The house used three wells since it had no running water, but within two or three days of moving, the motor to the backyard well was stolen. Next, three times in succession a thief sneaked in and made off with all his records. The thief had entered through the window, so Hideo had a lock installed; when the thief next came through the pivoted window above it he was caught. The prosecuting officer came to ask Hideo to write an affidavit to lighten the penalty, which Hideo did.

Some days later, a young man came, and Kiyomi inquired, "Who is it?"

"The thief who broke in the other day," came the reply, which startled Kiyomi. He had come to personally thank Hideo for the lightened penalty.

Wanting work, he asked Hideo to help him find a job, but no one would hire a thief. Finally with the help of poet-novelist Kuri Kikuoka, the thief became a longshoreman at Shibaura, but in no time disappeared after borrowing some money. Then also, some years later, three other thieves broke in, and struck Hideo on the cheek with a short sword, but he regained consciousness. He took out some money and began talking to them, which impressed one of the thieves so much that he lit Hideo's cigarette as they prepared to leave.

I heard later from Kiyomi that Haruko, their stout-hearted daughter, had slipped out of the house, ran a hundred yards to the house below and telephoned the police that thieves had broken in. Kiyomi praised her daughter's bravery and at the same time expressed how totally helpless she had been in her fright.

The three thieves too were later apprehended. When this made the newspapers, Hideo received a letter from the first thief of a few years earlier: "I am now married and settled. I read how some other thieves broke into your house. This brings to mind my past memories."

Chapter 24
How Deadly Boring It Is Talking To Men

Hideo scolded me many times, but I remember one occasion in particular after he had moved to the mountaintop house in 1948. Their small daughter, Haruko, had probably gone to bed, as she wasn't around. Hideo was sipping his evening sake, as Kiyomi and I were keeping him company. Our conversation turned to chatting about Seiichi Funabashi, who was then an active writer in popular magazines and newspapers. We began to comment about his two wives, how they strangely got along so well that they even enjoyed shopping together, when Hideo sharply reprimanded me: "Don't ridicule others. Christ said, 'Judge not others.'"

I cringed, sensing that he meant, "How can you, a Christian speak so about others?" Hideo never spoke ill of others behind their backs. If he had anything to say, it was straight to their face.

Kiyomi was then going through menopause. Each day she was irritable, anxious and lonely. She had hysterical fits and took tranquillisers and astraxin, so that Hideo said to her, "The problem is you think only about yourself. People who are lonely and anxious think only about themselves. You should think more of others. Think what you can do for others. Then your anxieties will disappear."

In such ways, Hideo admonished and reprimanded Kiyomi and me, yet without losing faith in women. He fully accepted women in spite of their foolishness and weaknesses. He had a magnanimity about him.

Hideo liked Hakuchō Masamune. Hideo said Hakuchō had always been a Christian deep in his heart, refuting the opinion of many that Hakuchō became a Christian in his youth, parted from the faith, and then returned to Christianity only late in life. He considered Hakuchō the most typical Christian Japanese since Kanzō Uchimura. Around two or three years before Hakuchō's death in 1962, he and Hideo were staying in the new wing of Kyoto's Miyako Hotel, when he confessed to Hideo his loneliness in not having a Bible to read. Though the Gideons Bible Society had provided Bibles in most major hotels in Japan by then, the new wing had not been so supplied.

Hakuchō quickly changed the topic, "I read the Bible only out of habit, after all." Hakuchō had felt embarrassed to talk openly about his Christian faith; this impressed Hideo. He commented that it indicated a natural feeling that the Japanese held, not a weakness of faith. Once again, Hideo showed his sensitivity in understanding people.

The writer Rinzō Shiina, a convert to Christianity, also wrote of feeling embarrassed about his immature faith while in church and about admitting his Christian faith outside of church. This, I believe, is an honest admission of a Japanese.

Once Hideo asked Hakuchō, "Who has influenced you the most?"

He contemplated and answered, "Perhaps my wife." It wasn't until around the age of seventy, however, that Hideo too began to feel the same way about Kiyomi, his wife.

I forget when, but Hideo once said to me, "How deadly boring it is talking to men. Men live in the conscious realm, but women in the unconscious world of Eros. However, so many women in the workforce today have put a lid on their Eros."

Hearing this, I thought how influenced men have been by the unconscious world of women's Eros. Though many have thought about the deep subtleties binding husbands and wives, few men like Hideo have managed to sense and express this. This subtlety of woman constitutes her strength, her weakness, her foolhardiness and her sadness. The other day when I was watching TV, I heard the actress Isuzu Yamada admit that she tried to act feminine on stage, but her real self also yearned to be a woman. She thought that a woman's quintessence was a natural trait endowed from god, natural to the life of a woman.

I have a small ring that reminds me of Hideo whenever I look at it. When I wear it, in all the sincerity of a woman I feel a joy that enriches my heart. Actually both Hideo and my husband had enabled me to possess this rare, valuable ring.

It was around 1956 or 1957. I had visited the mountaintop house one day, when Hideo showed me this ring. It was a curious pure gold ring of simple design, set with a blackish-red garnet as broad as my finger. The surface of the garnet was inscribed with two rows of ancient hieroglyphics. The thin ring was small and oblong and barely fit the little finger on my left hand. Both Kiyomi and Haruko sitting next to me shouted, "It fits, it fits!" The small ring had not fit their little fingers.

Hideo explained that the ring had been excavated in Tehran and dated back to almost 300 A.D. The small and thin ring appeared to be a child's. Since he liked the shape and design, he had purchased it for either Kiyomi or Haruko.

Hideo said to me, "Since it fits you perfectly, I'll sell it to you." I was relieved that he said it so willingly.

Worried about the price of such an expensive ring, nonetheless I wore it home. My husband, impressed with it after a careful look, offered it as my Christmas present. That really thrilled me.

As for the inscription, we could not determine whether it was Greek or Latin. Hideo surmised that the inscription was the name of a child, but even two or three theologians could not decipher it.

A few years later in the late fifties I went to America and I met many Christian women, who inquired, "Why aren't you wearing a wedding ring?"

Each time, my reply was that I had offered the ring to Japan's war efforts; they would nod, saying, "I see", showing some pity. I said then that I instead wore the garnet ring, which I showed them on my finger. I inquired if anyone could read the hieroglyphics and had some American scholars look at it. This was inconclusive, since the hieroglyphics were unclear. Some said the Hebrew reading meant Israel, and others said it meant Jesus Christ.

Hideo received many outstanding awards in Japan. In 1953 he received the Yomiuri Literary Award for his book *Van Gogh's Letters*. Next, in 1958 he received the Noma Literary Arts Award for his book *Modern Paintings*. My husband and I were invited to the award ceremony and heard Hideo's acceptance speech.

> I wondered how I should spend this award money. Since I enjoyed every minute writing *Modern Paintings*, I thought of spending the money on some enjoyment and not on something for my moral improvement. Going to an earthenware exhibition the other day, I spotted an attractive small clay figurine and asked the price. It was fifty million yen, some fifty times the amount of the award of one million yen, so I had to forgo the idea. Starting up golf recently, I had purchased an expensive set of golf clubs. I thought anything expensive must be good, but the handles turned out to be too long. So with this award money, I have decided to buy a new set of golf clubs.

Everyone burst out laughing, a most appropriate greeting for such a gala occasion.

The next year, in 1959, Hideo was selected as a member of the Fine Arts' Committee. For the occasion, since four were invited for a night's stay at Hakone, I gladly went when Hideo invited us. Hideo, Kiyomi, Haruko, and I went to spend a leisurely night, which I believe was at Fujiya Hotel in Miyanoshita. This was the only occasion I ever travelled with the three members of the Kobayashi family.

Then four years later, in 1963, Hideo received the Cultural Achievement Award, and again four years later, in 1967, the Order of Culture, Japan's most prestigious award. He was the youngest recipient that year, at the age of sixty-five.

Around that season, colourful autumn leaves dotted the late autumn scene that enveloped the mountaintop house; "sazanka" camellia flowers were blooming in the yard. Kiyomi happened to show me the gorgeous photo album presented to Hideo and Kiyomi at the Culture Award Ceremony, which included a large photo taken at the Emperor's Palace. They were the youngest of the group beyond a doubt. Moreover, even to his last days, Hideo never seemed to age during our talks together. Also in those days, Hideo and Kiyomi never spoke to one another as if they were old.

I was looking at the large photo when Kiyomi said, "At the Emperor's Palace, I spoke to the other wives and how admirable they all were. They all had contributed so much to their husband's achievements. Only I, in my mediocrity, had done so little."

Then Hideo replied, "Yes, you are so mediocre." I sensed a tone of affection in this. Hideo later did agree with Hakuchō that his wife had been the most influential person in his life. I believe that the genuine are those who admit their wrongs, claim that they are unable to do good and are undeserving—which is a biblical teaching—rather than those who claim to do good, to be honest and to have suffered for others. This resembles the pure heartedness that Hakuchō indicated as he shamefully admitted his loneliness when finding himself without a Bible in the Kyoto hotel. This purity (on the decline today) has long influenced others and responded to the feelings of others.

I sensed in Hideo and Kiyomi this kind of affection for each other, although they never talked about it.

Then in June 1978 Hideo received the Japan Literary Prize for his book *Motoori Norinaga*. The acceptance speech at the award presentation, which appeared in the newspaper, seemed so appropriate.

> Any book must sell. This idea was basic to Motoori Norinaga who, as a physician, excelled at publicizing his home-concocted "jiyōgan" pills. Learning this from Norinaga, I have publicized the book, in which the sentences are so improvised that one must read on, stop, then turn back. The reader finds himself reading it two or three times over. It sells for 4,000 yen; but if you consider the length, then it is worth 12,000 yen and so is quite a bargain.

Since our father's grave was located at Saifukuji Temple at Shi-no-hashi, Minato ward, when he died in 1921, our mother's ashes were also buried there in 1946. Hideo and I, however, rarely visited the grave except for the Seventh Memorial Year or other ceremonies. It was Kiyomi who visited the grave every year during the equinoctial week and during the *obon* season. I had accompanied her only a few times.

This had been on Hideo's mind. Later in life he went to Tōkeiji Temple near Kita-Kamakura Station to visit the family grave of the cartoonist Ryōsuke Nasu, with whom Hideo often played golf, ate and travelled. He found a quiet spot surrounded by solemn, tall trees, where he considered transferring the family grave. Tōkeiji Temple, however, was an old Zen temple of some repute and history among the Magome temples, so the graveyard as expected had no space left. Hideo was downhearted, but he kept walking around persistently until he spotted an area below a mountain embankment, where a tiny stream flowed down and the trees with tinted leaves grew tall. He requested that the embankment be dug out and the ground levelled to make space, and the understanding temple master approved.

For the gravestone there, Hideo transferred the small five-storied pagoda, purchased after the war in a Kansai curio shop. The old pagoda of the Kamakura period, his most beloved item, was placed in the yard.

Finally on 6 August 1977, a hot summer day, our parents' remains were transferred from Saifukuji Temple to Tōkeiji Temple. The Kobayashi family, the Nasu and Takamizawa couples gathered there.

At the main sanctuary, the head priest offered prayers before our parents' remains, after which Kiyomi said, "You carry your mother's urn to the grave site."

I thanked Kiyomi for her thoughtfulness, since I—a negligent daughter —felt this was the least I could do to repay my mother. Hideo went ahead of me with father's urn, and I followed carrying mother's urn to the grave while apologizing silently that I had not visited their graves more often. Hideo perhaps shared the same feeling.

The burial ceremony ended, and so did the priest's short prayer. We took turns offering incense, then poured the water of purification over the pagoda gravestone, when Hideo standing behind us said, "To this site, I too can frequently come to pay them my respects."

Chapter 25
Because There Are Problems, So There Is Joy

Sometime after 10 June in the year Hideo died, a small package arrived from a former classmate of mine living in Hakodate, Hokkaido, who had deeply admired Hideo's writings since her college years.

The small package included two or three pressed, double-layer cherry blossoms placed neatly between white Japanese paper as well as a small, round Tupperware container which contained salt-preserved cherry blossoms to make a cherry blossom brew. She had some days earlier written to me explaining the blossoms. Their colours had been skilfully retained, and I looked at them fully appreciating her thoughtfulness.

Apparently she had read in an article of mine how deeply Hideo loved the double-layer blossoms called *fugenzō* that blossomed at his mountaintop house. This had surprised her since she had often seen this rare variety in Hokkaido.

The Matsumae Castle site, located at the southernmost tip of Hokkaido's Ōshima Peninsula, was noted for the beauty of its numerous cherry-blossom trees. Viewers swarmed there during the blossom season, but only after the crowds subsided in late May and the trees were covered in leaves did the *fugenzō* tree majestically bloom to gloriously mark the season's end. Brought from the ancient capital of Kyoto by a lady-in-waiting at the Matsumae Household, this *fugenzō* tree had since become well known in the area and was carefully protected.

Reading about Hideo's admiration for the double-layer blossoms, the friend resolved to see the blossoms in Matsumae that spring. But she heard that the unduly cold winter would delay the blossoming season, so she took her trip in early June, after which she wrote to me. All the cherry-blossom trees had grown leaves, except for the late-blooming *fugenzō* tree, whose petals fluttered and scattered to the ground. It was named *fugenzō* after the blossoms' centre, which resembled the nose of the elephant that Buddha had reportedly ridden on.

She walked to the lone shop, wanting to buy some picture postcards of the cherry-blossom tree. There were none, but the shopkeeper unexpectedly brought out some cherry-blossom brew. On top of this brew floated two beautiful delicate blossoms, whose sweet aroma she smelled as she brought her lips to the brew. She quickly asked, "Can I have a little more brew to take home?"

The shopkeeper regretfully replied that it was the last. Upon hearing this, she cherished sipping that *fugenzō* brew a mouthful at a time. Then she returned to the *fugenzō* tree, where she plucked off a few blossoms and brought them home to preserve in salt. Her letter let me know how it would please her if a cup of brew be made and placed in front of the photo of Hideo Kobayashi. Soon after, I brought the salt-preserved flowers to Kamakura.

After Hideo's death I received another letter, from a graduate student of Kokugakuin University in Tokyo, whom I had never met. He had read Hideo's works in high school and then in university but had found them incomprehensible. He nonetheless read on, feeling a compulsion to fathom Hideo's thoughts. Of course, he also read the *Complete Works*, commentaries on Hideo's works, as well as the works Hideo quoted from. They included works by Alain, Newton, William James, but particularly those by Bergson. He read them not as research on Hideo, but rather because he wanted to discover what Hideo demanded of himself in finding a way of life. His field of study was Japanese literature, but he had no ambition to do research on Hideo's writings or publishing a book on Hideo Kobayashi. He hoped to find himself.

Finally, in February 1980, he wrote to Hideo, wanting to see if his readings and response to Hideo's works were correct. He sought only to understand his works, feeling certain Hideo would read his letter. He had read (many times, he explained) a small book of mine written some years ago, describing how carelessly Hideo opened all the mail.

Now, two years after his death, I more fully admire Hideo. I now realize that few writers had so penetratingly read, grasped and written in so many fields as Hideo had. This I will write about later, but his inner struggle was intense, his sensitivity poignant, and his criticisms severe in all matters. Hideo had will power, intelligence and affection. Though he was critical, he loved people and showed his sympathy.

However, Hideo was terribly absent-minded and careless regarding matters unrelated to his work.

When he lived in the mountaintop house, he received many notices of gatherings, but often failed to reply. Whenever Kiyomi reminded him he replied, but would forget to designate whether he would attend and to write his name. I wrote in my small book how Hideo's daughter, Haruko, had angrily spoken about this hopeless trait of Hideo:

> Father is impossible. The other day he asked at the post office for ten postcards. Then he asked how much they cost. He should know

without having to ask. He thinks all the letters that come to the house are for him. He opens the letters and begins to read them. Halfway through, when a letter reads strangely, he hands it to me, saying it's for me. He should be ashamed.

The Kokugakuin University student had read this, feeling assured that Hideo would open his letter if he should write.

Whenever Hideo read anything, he read it well—though he rarely replied. Only when he felt it necessary to or when deeply moved did he answer. But he replied to this student's letter, a simple note on a postcard. Hideo apparently had been moved by the pure directness and honesty reflected in the student's letter.

The student was overjoyed to receive the postcard. His excitement did not subside until a week later. He explained to me how honoured he felt, coming all the way to my house in Machida city in Tokyo to tell me. Evidently Hideo's reply had helped him to develop his future self. In gratitude he showed me the postcard, carefully placed in a plastic train-pass holder. I read the very simple reply expressing Hideo's warmth and love for this young lad, whom he had never met.

> Thank you for your letter.
> Continue to read as you do.
> Take good care of yourself.
>
> Hideo Kobayashi

In my Hokkaido friend and this student, I see Hideo's figure at work even after his death. As I look at the photo of Hideo in my room, the words "The deceased are forgotten, as the days pass" seem contradictory. Hideo is ever closer to me. However, he is unable to reply to my bidding, so a new sadness comes over me.

At gatherings and meetings I attend, I hear people repeatedly quoting Hideo, or I hear references to his works—even at occasions unrelated to literature or publications. There are others too, including successful publishers, who tell me of their gratitude for Hideo's help—even though Hideo had reprimanded them in their youth.

Also, over ten years ago, I met a young, successful minister in a small town in the Tōhoku area, who said, "I wanted to meet Mr Kobayashi and thank him. I had enrolled in a seminary but considered dropping out, having fallen into doubt and disillusionment. Then by chance I read Mr Kobayashi's works, which fascinated me. While reading his collected works, I felt awakened. I resumed my study, then decided to become a minister. This decision was best, for which I have Mr Kobayashi to thank. I wanted to do this at least once."

This minister had found himself in Hideo's writings. He may have happened upon Hideo's words, "Man can genuinely believe only what Christ experienced in life, and the record of this written in the Bible by his disciples who believed in their experiences."

His decision to become a minister after reading Hideo's writings is not at all strange. Hideo himself sought truth all through his life, writing on the true way of life and values for the genuine person.

Hideo struggled to establish a niche for criticism and for critics of literature in Japan. From a mere appendage to novels and essays, criticism became a respectable new genre for aesthetic writing. However, Hideo never wrote criticism with this in mind. He himself says:

> When I began writing essays, I did not intend them to become criticisms. I wrote what I felt as I liked, which turned out to be criticism. Without tiring, I merely continued on.

Hideo wrote as he liked on what he liked. How fortunate he was. But people remark on the ease of this task. Actually, it was far more challenging to do so. He enjoyed writing, but he faced countless barriers. Hideo knew it was necessary to overcome them for the writing to be genuine.

He used to say, "Only through suffering, one finds true joy. Because there are problems, so there is joy."

He also said to me, "Doing the enjoyable without facing hardships is not doing it oneself. Another is doing it while one's own hands are in one's pockets. What is enjoyable entails trials and difficulties."

I agreed, "One must untiringly continue to write anything worthy."

Jun'ichirō Sako, the writer and educator, once said, "Writers all face problems. But Hideo Kobayashi struggled to the extreme. I once caught a glimpse of him writing at an inn. He was on all fours crawling around the straw-mat room."

Around 1955, Hideo evidently remarked to a young writer dashing off articles for journalistic publications, "You dash off articles on request, but fail as a craftsman writer. A craftsman reflects on whatever he finds distasteful. For example, he will dash to pieces his own works that are not to his satisfaction."

Hideo liked the craftsman spirit, saying, "I too am a kind of craftsman." It was in this spirit that he wrote.

However, few qualify as craftsman writers, painters and creative artists as Hideo described. I feel as if I have been struck on the head by his words. I write my manuscripts with difficulty and, because I lack the courage to refuse, I accept every request. After beginning to write, I run into a mental block, feeling the pressure of a deadline, which brings me to tears. Of course, I submit my writings even though they do not satisfy me. I never accept only the writing I want to do, and take time over, struggle to write and then, if I don't like it, throw it away. Hideo held standards far above mine.

He re-read and re-wrote, reducing the length of his manuscripts. Writers like me tend to make additions when we re-read the manuscript, increasing the number of pages. When Hideo was writing the monthly series "Motoori Norinaga", the pages decreased from the original ten manuscript pages to three. So concise and compact, what others wrote in half a page, he said in two or three lines. He took great pains to select words, devise the sentences, and improve the expression. Thus his writing became increasingly complex to read, but its words bore weight like poetry—as expressed by the phrase "It is a criticism of poetry and, at the same time, a poetry of criticism."

Chapter 26
Writing Criticism Cultivates Oneself

Though some accused Hideo of dogmatism, a juggler of paradoxes and a tactician of style, his writings continue to be unique and highly individualistic.

All quality works imbue a uniqueness peculiar to the writer, on which Hideo comments:

> Most people regard unsociable and egocentric loners who lack common sense as strong-willed individualists. But they are self-centred, not strong-willed individualists. Individuality develops not according to one's will, but to the degree one is involved in society with a gentle and meek heart. Society moulds individuality. Being extremely humble, even prepared to deny himself, Van Gogh produced highly individualistic works. You must possess a naiveté, so that when you meet someone more gifted than yourself you can respect that person from deep within your heart. Conducting oneself impartially and trusting in others effectively develops individuality. All other efforts in seeking uniqueness cannot produce creative works.

Within this paradox Hideo conducted himself and sought to develop his individuality, which is reflected in his works as a critic.

Hideo often wrote on criticism itself, particularly on the spirit of criticism, which I believe few have probed as deeply as he. I don't think I've delved deeply into criticism. Works like those I've written are often criticized, and every time this happens I realize how difficult true criticism is, that true criticism is as Hideo says. I am led to agree with Hideo on what constitutes truth, which he says must include a metaphysical aspect.

Hideo often wrote on poetry cards "Writing criticism is the path to non-self."

"Achieving non-self means submitting to nature but, furthermore, recognizing a greater power than oneself. Losing oneself in it means submitting to the Great Soul."

One must understand this to write worthwhile criticism that is premised on love.

Hideo also said, "Criticism without love is 'mistaken'. One must love, believe and like what one criticizes in order to write good criticism."

Hideo came to like Hakuchō Masamune after he learned how intimately and fondly Hakuchō read the works of others. Hideo himself admitted that he wrote his best criticism when praising others; he said that the spirit of criticism consisted of this, rather than of denouncing others, which is contrary to the spirit of criticism. Of course, by "praise" he meant sincere praise, not empty flattery or superficial remarks.

Regarding Hideo's spirit of criticism, I further quote from his various writings, but not without risks. For example, when we quote short Bible verses and add our arbitrary comments, we only deviate from the original and later sense a gloom. Hideo too knew these difficulties well.

Hideo was writing the series "Dostoevsky" when a cynical critic commented: "To earn his keep, a strange critic quotes directly from Dostoevsky's works that fill his ten pages or so in magazine articles."

Hideo wrote about another instance in his essay "Kokugo to iu Taiga" (The Large River of the Japanese Language; 1958):

> One day, my daughter showed me her Japanese language test, saying that one part made no sense. I read it, thinking it badly written. I instructed her to write her teacher that it was impossible to work out what it meant. My daughter started to laugh. That "question" was taken from your father's book, her teacher had told her. "Oh really," I said, dumbfounded. Just when I had thought that I had become like complaining Kogoto Kōbei, I had lost face.... Another day, someone from a newspaper office in the province called. He said the local school had included my writings in their entrance exam, but the PTA was in an uproar over the ambiguities. He desired to publish the correct answer provided by the writer, so he began to read tediously over the phone a piece I had written years ago. Listening, I became increasingly exasperated. "The accurate meaning is ... "; "Yes, that's right"; "Read it as is". Slam! I hung up. I remember this happening. It only irritated both sides.

It is futile to fully understand a piece of writing when limited to reading only one small part. One comprehends only by reading the entire context. Admittedly, Hideo's quotes on criticism from scattered sources fail as a full commentary, but they can provide the reader with a general understanding. So I have gathered some quotes, including some comments from our conversations together.

> Before writing criticism, first make sure you recognize the worthiness of the writer. With all the flexibility of your non-self, grasp him for what he is. Begin your task by losing yourself, then you can clearly see that person.
>
> Some say, "Because one is assertive, one must be critical. Being assertive is productive, but being critical can be negative and non-productive." However, a pure spirit of criticism plays down not only assertions, but also all standpoints of assertions.
>
> Most crucial is to rid oneself of biases. By so doing, we grasp what is true; or, rather, the truth grasps us.
>
> The ultimate nature of criticism is to recognize that a person differs in values and to respect him all the same. Writing criticism is not scholarship or research, but a process of cultivating one's self.

In this spirit of warm love, Hideo read the works of others seriously.

As already mentioned, Hideo wrote dense prose, compressing his sentences to make his writings difficult. Hideo said that anyone who reads them many times over would surely understand. "A person who truly loves a writer and his works will endure re-reading them. I have always done this with all great works."

Since his higher-school days, Hideo read most of Dostoevsky's works and harboured him in his heart. His works continued to engross him for ten years, until his marriage in 1934, when Hideo actually began writing his series on Dostoevsky that continued to 1939. His interest continued for another thirty-one years, until the 1960s. Around 1936, he said:

> Instead of discussing the importance of Dostoevsky as a person, my criticism has centred on "describing" him. I have developed this confidence in me... and thoroughly enjoyed myself. Only how he appeared and lived mattered to me.

In his book *Hideo Kobayashi*, Jun Etō compares Hideo's image of Dostoevsky with that of E. H. Carr's *Dostoevsky*. He says "Carr's protagonist walks the streets of Petersburg, whereas Kobayashi's strolls inside his heart." This suggests how thoroughly Dostoevsky had possessed Hideo.

Around 1936, Hideo saw the movie *Crime and Punishment* produced by the French director Pierre Chenal. After the title sequence, a portrait of Dostoevsky was projected onto the large theatre screen. When Hideo opened the door to enter, he imagined that Dostoevsky himself was seated inside, and tears came to his eyes. Hideo wanted the scene to last longer, and when it changed, he said he considered leaving the theatre. Hideo showed no interest in the movie. Because he was disturbed, the good cast and skilled performance of this masterpiece left no mark on him. Only the portrait of Dostoevsky had moved him.

For thirty years, from 1933 to the 1960s, Hideo wrote and lectured on Dostoevsky. He had never been to Russia but yearned to see the Kiev River and visit Dostoevsky's grave. The trip was finally realized in 1963 at the invitation of the Russian Writers' Association. Thereafter, he no longer felt his work on Dostoevsky complete, but felt he was no longer able to write on him. Perhaps he got too close, overly attached to him.

Hideo read voluminously in so many fields that it amazed people. I found out that he also read the Bible, often including the Old Testament.

I previously wrote about Hideo's carelessness, which Hidemi Kon also describes. Early in Hideo's career, he visited Kon's house and so often kicked over his teacup on the straw mat as he stood up that it seemed almost intentional. Or he would open the nearest door, forgetting that Japanese houses had their restrooms at the end of the hallway. Then he would forget again, proceed to kick over his teacup and go to open the wrong door again.

When I visited Hideo's home in Kamakura one day, he took out a sake cup from a paulownia box and started to drink sake from it. But as he stood up and started to walk, he stepped on and broke the box. When I started to pick up the pieces, I noticed some writing on one of the pieces. Fitting the pieces together, I was able to read:

> I am young in years,
> And you are elderly,
> Therefore, I was timid and afraid.
>
> —Hideo—

Apparently he had written it with a brush in his younger days. I forget when and why he selected these words, but I remembered that he mentioned a young Old Testament prophet. Later I discovered that they came from Elihu's words in the Book of Job. Job said that Elihu was correct and silenced Job's three friends. Elihu, the youngest, said these words in anger at Job and his three elders. When he lived at the hillside Ōgigayatsu house, a woodblock print by William Blake hung on the wall. It depicted three or four people and a winged angelic figure, with Bible verses filling the space between. The above three lines appeared near the centre of the picture. Blake's woodblock print apparently depicted the story of Job, in which a passage read:

> And Elihu the son of Barachel the Buzite answered: "I am young in years, and you are elderly; therefore, I was timid and afraid to declare my opinion to you."

Hideo wrote profusely, read widely, and perceived keenly. That he perceived keenly meant that he looked with the heart and saw what escaped the physical eyes.

Hideo's eye for painting led to his great admiration for Van Gogh's works. Around 1948 Hideo went to a classical painting exhibition in Ueno, Tokyo, where he saw a replica of "Crows in the Wheat Field" by Van Gogh, painted just before the artist committed suicide (1890). Without much knowledge of painting, he was stunned by this rare painting, which forced him to squat down paralyzed before the painting.

Hideo powerfully describes this painting:

> The orchestra suddenly pauses, a flock of crows silently flies off, and shadows of figures as if from the Old Testament disappear behind the stalks of wheat. This did not seem entirely right for the canvas. Far behind it, a Giant Eye was staring at me, which paralyzed me.

Wanting that replica, he inquired about the owner's name whenever meeting art dealers. The writer Chiyo Uno perhaps heard about this, found the painting and sent it to Hideo. Hideo was overjoyed, but became unable to rid himself of a desire that possessed his mind, an annoying urge to discover what [Van Gogh's] Giant Eye meant. The excitement he felt then never left him and, after wondering what to do, he decided he had to write about it. An inspiration that cannot be described is a lie, he believed. So Hideo began writing his series "Letters of Van Gogh".

He had to express in writing that Great Something, lurking invisibly in Van Gogh's masterpiece.

Not only with paintings, but regarding all things, Hideo explained the process of seeing: "Only the eye of the heart can see history. The physical eye cannot see history, since a truly perceptive person sees what lies behind."

The eye of the heart meant that the heart saw. The heart referred to imaginative powers of warm affection. One must see with the heart, not with the eyes.

Hideo quotes Henri Bergson: "Man sees not because one has eyes. Man sees in spite of having eyes." That is, the physical eye interferes with the process of the eye of the heart. Georges Rouault of France says, similarly, "How pitiful the human eye. Once it begins to look, it no longer sees."

Man boasts, saying, "I saw it with my own eyes", but his physical eyes often perceive what is not true.

I had ignored his words before, but some words from Hideo only now make sense to me:

> To see is extremely difficult. For the writer, seeing is like feeling ceramic ware, a process that differs from that of a photographer. We see

as if leisurely caressing objects. The moving hands find life in the seeing process.

In a warm love for the ceramics, the moving hands enliven the seeing process, I believe.

The affectionate care with which Hideo read works, saw items and wrote criticism impresses us—but, by contrast, he was also extremely careless.

Hideo's family consisted of three, until the marriage of his daughter in 1965. Until then each had a designated towel and toothbrush, always totalling three. It was very clear, but Hideo often used the wrong one.

Also, the straw-mat room at the mountaintop house had fixed sliding doors for a wall, which resembled those of a large walk-in closet, probably to add cosiness to the room. After nearly twenty years there, one day he tried to open the doors then he realized, "Oh, I remember, it doesn't open."

Then, perhaps on a lecture trip, he had jumped onto a train and looked out onto the platform, noticing some suitcases. He thought they looked familiar as the train started to move out. Only after the suitcases were out of sight did he realize that they were his.

Another example was when I stayed overnight at Hideo's. I was about to leave for home, when I couldn't find my glasses that I had left in the living room. I looked for them in the straw-mat room and the kitchen without success. Kiyomi promised to send them when she found them, and I returned to the living room to bid Hideo farewell. Looking at him as he sat reading the newspapers, I found he was wearing my glasses! How could he read wearing someone else's glasses that had a different focal lens?

Then also, during Hideo and Hidemi Kon's travels in Europe, Hideo lost many things. He forgot his light-exposure gauge among the ruins in Egypt, his camera in a taxi in Rome and many lighters at various places. In order for Hideo not to forget, Hidemi Kon advised him to place all his items in his pockets—which Hideo did. Leaving Milano, Italy, and finally arriving at a Florence hotel, Hideo took out the items from his pockets—whereupon he removed his room key to the Milano Hotel.

Chapter 27
Each Must Believe In His Own Way

"Without a notion of Eternity, I believe, there can be no art or morality." Hideo thought about eternity and believed in an Absolute that he termed the Great Soul.

Even today we see many strange phenomena and irrationalities that Hideo had the frankness to admit were inexplicable.

Thus he believed in the supernatural.

He said, "There is Something Great in which I exist. So my heart moves in a way that this Something Great does. I find this natural and cannot do otherwise. Modern thought, however, suggests that this Something Great is unnatural."

Hideo lamented that the new generation was unable to respond to a God, or Something Great. Hideo believed in an omnipotent Invisible Power that transcended man.

After writing on Dostoevsky for some seven years, he wrote around 1940: "This genius said he found 'inspiration' the essence of his writing"—he wrote this again some twenty years later. Around that time, in 1963, the word inspiration, almost unheard today, was often used in a popular sense, but carelessly so. We used it disregarding the word's deeper significance—as the solemnity of spirituality, a godly enlightenment, and a response to the divine.

In April of 1963, Hideo wrote in a newspaper essay:

> Not long ago, aesthetes relished the word inspiration, but today it has been prostituted into staleness. People today do not allow for ambiguities such as the spiritual in aesthetics, confining themselves to the conscious realm. Most think that the age when an undeveloped analytic consciousness relied upon inspiration in its work has passed. So-called progressive ideas on art do not facilitate the path for aesthetes to produce masterpieces. It is interesting that this is so. We use words of the ancients in our own modern interpretations. The ancients used the word inspiration in quite a different way. It is not difficult for me to

focus my spirit in order to prepare my consciousness, using my expertise in the same way as craftsmen use their expertise. What should follow? Just wait. An idea comes to mind from somewhere. I put words together, then send orders to my consciousness. Like the ancients, I wait for this so-called old-fashioned sort of inspiration.

Hideo knew that man's ability and talents were limited, and thereby believed in a Great Power that transcended man, or what we call the gods.

"It is our heavenly-endowed gifts that transcend man's power and that produce masterpieces," he used to say.

In his book *Mozart*, Hideo also quotes Mozart:

> An idea appears in our souls very fresh, flowing like a stream. However, we do not know from where it comes or how it appears. Far beyond the reach of even my small finger.... Once the idea is formed, I cannot readily forget it. This probably is the gods' supreme gift to me.

Even the Nobel Prize winner, the scientist Hideki Yukawa, who discovered the mesotron, said: "I find discoveries and inventions are born as enlightenment from Heaven, not from a compilation of theories or performing countless experiments."

Also, Hideo once told me:

> Regardless of our efforts, we cannot see electrons or neutrons. Similarly, man seeking to comprehend or see the gods only compels them into hiding. Man can never know the gods this way, but the gods nonetheless exist. We cannot know the gods from without, but must enter and unite with the gods. To be one with the gods means to love them. Sensing the beauty of flowers means to love them. When feeling the flower's beauty, one enters, unites with and loves it. In contrast to merely seeing or viewing, love enables one to enter and become one with the flower.

Becoming one means unconditionally accepting, believing in and respecting it in its entirety—and loving it. This is faith in Christianity.

Hideo also said to me: "To understand eternal life in Christianity is difficult, but a true believer should display full joy in his life. Why doesn't that joy show in you?"

Not only I, but few Christians show this joy simply and innocently like a child. We fall into Christian mannerisms and fail to unite in oneness with God. Hideo speaks of a loving God that has become so vague we no longer sense His love for us.

One believer said, "Believing that God exists is not the Christian faith, but believing God loves me is."

I believe that Hideo's words "Become one with God" are the same as this. This enables us to sense His great love for us foolish human beings and feel joy. But we fail in this.

Hideo also said: "Christians must find more joy in death than in living." This is true for one with deep faith. Hideo rebuked me, since my faith was weak, particularly in my first ten years as a Christian. I remember Hideo instructing me as if he were a minister.

I had once explained to Hideo about Jun'ichirō Sako, a former editor at Sōgensha and Kadokawa publishers, who later became a Christian minister, "Before writing, Mr Sako first places his manuscript paper on his desk and prays. Then he begins to write. But he is actually doing the writing with his own talents. I don't think he needs to pray."

Unexpectedly, Hideo scolded me, "He doesn't need to pray? Not so. The Bible says, 'Pray without ceasing', doesn't it? It's only natural to. How wrong to assume that one can achieve by himself. Man is limited regardless of his efforts. All effort can fall short, so man must ask for God's strength by praying to the Omnipotent. Without this, what can man achieve?"

His words hit home. How true, I thought, impressed by Mr Sako's faith. As for myself, to this day I neglect to pray before writing. I simply forget to, and perhaps for this reason, my writing leaves much to be desired.

Hideo saw well my lacklustre faith, and said: "How can you judge people as either believers or non-believers? Do you know what true faith is? Can you confidently say your faith is genuine?"

Hideo's words brought to mind what a university professor wrote some years ago:

> At a certain Christian seminar, about twenty active Christians, ministers, university teachers and writers met, and to my surprise their beliefs all differed—even on the oneness of the Trinity and the Resurrection. Some, like the writers Rinzō Shiina and Kazuo Kitamori, were experientialist orthodox Christians; and others were practising Calvinists even in this day and age. All varied, some believing that the Resurrection was a vision, and others claiming to be enlightened by both Christianity and Buddhism, holding to a broad, existential stance. Still others adhered to both the Buddhist dogmas and the Gospels. I strongly felt that each needed to begin by looking into his own faith.

Perhaps, only the Almighty knows what faith is. Hideo puts it this way:

> To believe means believing in a unique way. To know means knowing as all others do. There are these two paths. To know is always scholarly: "I know, but you don't know. So that approach is wrong."

However, to believe means "Since I myself believe, my beliefs differ from yours."

From his middle-school years, Hideo had read Dostoevsky's works. But it was not until his thirties that he lost himself in Dostoevsky's works—re-reading, studying and enjoying Dostoevsky's works as he wrote on Dostoevsky. Hideo says that he had learned much about Christianity. How diligently he must have read the Bible along with Dostoevsky's works during those ten years.

Hideo concludes each of his works "Dosutoefuskii no Seikatsu" (Life of Dostoevsky; 1937) and *"Tsumi to Batsu* ni Tsuite" (On *Crime and Punishment*; 1948) with two beautiful poems from the Bible.

> I, the biographer, must end the sketch of his life with his death. His thoughts, or rather, at least my thoughts in which I attempt to revive him, must end with his death. It is an appropriate time today to read "his restless, uncommon works". That is, his life near the end seemed peaceful, but his spirit was in turmoil. Dostoevsky must have known Paul's words: "For if we are beside ourselves, it is for God; if we are in our right mind, it is for you." —II Corinthians 5:13—
>
> Raskolnikov was neither lonely when put in jail nor anxious about having killed a woman. The shadows bear the abnormal scene (which is the real abnormality) that bespeaks of human loneliness and anxiety. Those who see this, let them see. Those who see can no longer ignore the title *Crime and Punishment*, which Dostoevsky does not comment on even once. However, those who hear, let them hear: "... for whatever does not proceed from faith is sin". —Romans 14:23—

In 1950 at the age of forty-eight, Hideo wrote:

> I was asked my opinion on the topic "Can religion save mankind?" It is a question beyond me, so for me to answer....
> I can think as others do, which would be most convincing—but each must believe in his own way for genuine faith. For this reason, I suppose the act of faith, as opposed to thought, exists.
> If asked "Do I have a belief?" rather than "Can religion save mankind?" I would answer in the affirmative. If asked "Can my belief save me?" I would answer, "I don't know."

As Hideo says, discussions regarding faith become intricate since the nuances of "save" vary, each person having his own interpretation.

In April 1963, some Christians founded the magazine *Shinto no Tomo* (Believers' Companion), with Jun'ichirō Sako as chief editor, and Hideo agreed to an interview with him for the July issue.

In the interview, Editor Sako claims that Dostoevsky did not seek Christ's salvation, but rather Christ sought him—with which Hideo agrees.

> Although this was clear to himself, others failed to understand this and some aspects of Dostoevsky's confessions. Other people may make various comments [on Dostoevsky], but the fact is, a certain power had enabled him to create such writings. He produced works from a religious experience, not from an ordeal of his own volition to search.

Next, Hideo claims that truth and beauty unite in Dostoevsky's understanding of Greek Orthodoxy and that *The Idiot*, Mushkin, is Dostoevsky's image of Christ. The Russian words for truth and beauty are identical, so for Dostoevsky Christ becomes the world's most beautiful figure. Hideo also said that religion vis-à-vis aesthetics remains an important problem, but Plato had already united truth, goodness and beauty. This relates to Confucius's thoughts. Motoori Norinaga, too, in his ideas does not pit truth against beauty, rather they are placed within the realm of the gods and Heavenly Respect. That is, beauty is truth.

Chapter 28
Where Human Emotions Are Absent, So Are Truth, Beauty And Faith

In October 1974, Professor Hideo Ōki of the Tokyo Theological University wrote an article titled "'Ogorazaru Hitomo Hisashi Karazu' no Setsu ni Tsuite: Shingakuteki Kobayashi Hideo Ron" (On 'The Prideless Will Also Fall': The Theological Views of Hideo Kobayashi) for *Eureka* magazine's special issue on Hideo Kobayashi. It was a short nine-page article, but it was impressive. It was not only well written, but also penetrated into Hideo's religious beliefs to a depth that had escaped my notice.

I had often heard of Hideo Ōki, the foremost Japanese theologian, but I had never met him. When he was preparing to write the article, we met and spoke on familiar terms.

I simply told him of my experiences with Hideo, and what I knew and thought about Hideo's ideas. The beginning of the article describes our meeting.

> Something about his sister impressed me as she talked about her brother. How beautiful their relationship was. It was so beautifully impressive.... Talking with Ms Takamizawa, I felt Hideo Kobayashi's idea of transience prompting me to write this article. How was I to understand this idea of his? We discussed in depth Kobayashi's words "The prideless will also fall", a topic Ms Takamizawa had apparently lectured on somewhere. The above aroused in me a new interest in Hideo Kobayashi's writings, and I felt a strong attachment to him.

That Professor Ōki had described my relationship with Hideo as beautiful was a little embarrassing, since I had never thought it so. He may have detected something beautiful in my deep respect for Hideo.

Dōkan Ōta had replied, "The prideless will also fall", to his father's reprimand "Pride comes before a fall like a dream in spring." This is an anecdote recorded in the *Heike Tales*. Hitherto this was interpreted as "the prosperous inevitably fall" or "all is flowing and impermanent", which Hideo took to task in his essay "My View of Life" (1948):

> The story goes that youthful Dōkan Ōta had displayed so much pride that his distressed father wrote in brush "Pride comes before a fall" to caution him. Then, in quick response, Dōkan took the brush and wrote after it, "The prideless will also fall."

Hideo contends that the words "All is flowing and impermanent" had long been mistakenly interpreted to mean "All phenomena are in flux and without permanence". The latter part—"without permanence"—he asserts should read without heart, meaning: rules without heart or, to put it another way, dogmas that forget humanity. These, man had found hard to accept and confront directly, and had sought meaning elsewhere.

While discussing without heart, Ōki's essay takes up Hideo's religious beliefs, which I wish to explain. But before I do, I must mention another article, "The Religious Faith of Hideo Kobayashi", written by Keiichi Sakuta for the same issue of *Eureka* magazine.

According to Sakuta, Raskolnikov in *Crime and Punishment* finally hid the stolen valuables under a rock the day following his horrid crime. He is absentmindedly wandering about when he is almost run down by a horse-drawn buggy and is whipped across the back. A woman sees this and, mistaking him for a tramp, hands him twenty kopeck silver coins. From the bridge, the view of Kiev River is breathtaking. From here he tosses the silver into the river. Why? Dostoevsky does not explain, because he believes in something beyond reason. Had Raskolnikov thought himself unworthy of receiving any mercy? Had he expressed his complete solitude, cut off from all forms of existence, including God? Had he foreseen a coming, a metaphysical sort of punishment? All explanation eludes understanding. The first to point out the importance of this was Kobayashi, says Professor Sakuta. Then Kobayashi's ingenuity discovers a deep meaning here, which relates closely to his faith, Sakuta explains:

> Kobayashi speaks of a faith outside any established religion. The source of all religions, which man is apt to forget, consists of man's primitive, human experience. This is more than faith: it is more accurately the will to believe. Kobayashi has attracted numerous readers over many years because he had for decades referred to this will in earnest.

Although Sakuta is convincing, since Hideo denied being Buddhist or Christian and refused to believe in religions, saying they were man-made I feel that Hideo believed in something more than a subjective abstract will to believe, in something outside himself; it was something more objectively concrete. Though Hideo warned me against commenting on others' beliefs, he always used to say,

> Something beyond is always pressing upon me.
>
> Unless one believes, life is worthless and meaningless.

Also, he had said to me many times,

> Man can genuinely believe only what Christ experienced in life, and the record of this written in the Bible by his disciples who believed in their experiences.
>
> The Bible instructs neither knowledge nor scholarship. Nothing rational. Some read the Bible as moral instructions, but it is more. Records of religious experiences cannot be capriciously interpreted. It is filled with words of heartfelt human emotions, so important for mankind. It teaches that human feelings are most vital for life. This is true. Since the Bible contains truth, people read it.

Finally, he had said to me often,

> Where human emotions are absent, so are truth, beauty and faith.

The new genre of criticism—spirit of "non-self"—founded by Hideo was more Christian in spirit than simply religious. Only through his firm belief in Christ, the gods or an Absolute could he make such concrete, truth-filled statements.

Hideo's "spirit of criticism" meant this: "To properly write criticism, one must become non-self. One must get rid of the self. Only then does one grasp truth or, better put, what is truth grasps hold of one."

Furthermore, he firmly believed: "To lose one's self is to submit to the Great Soul."

Now we return to Professor Ōki's essay which begins with a quote from Hideo's essay "Gohho no E" (Van Gogh's Paintings; 1962). After being so absorbed with Dostoevsky, Hideo became infatuated with van Gogh for about ten years, this time from around the age of forty-six. Then he wrote on van Gogh, which again involved Christianity and the Bible.

Also, for another ten years, Hideo was infatuated with Roualt. However, in his last twenty years Motoori Norinaga had also possessed Hideo. I see Hideo's alter ego and his spirit in the writer Norinaga and the artist Rouault. Also in both, I see his faith.

Perhaps because he liked them, he came to resemble them; or because he resembled them, he came to like them. Whichever is the case, he entered the writer and the artist, both of whom he loved, becoming one with them.

Professor Ōki quotes from Hideo's essay "Van Gogh's Paintings":

Van Gogh aspired to be a pastor before becoming a painter. First, Christ possessed him, then he became disillusioned and disappointed with an evangelist's life; he then attempted to fulfil his aspirations on canvas. He sought in painting to unite his religious and aesthetic impulses, an accomplishment he found impossible in the times he lived in.

Then Ōki claims that Hideo Kobayashi, too, sought to unite the religious with the aesthetic, probing with a depth that seems to resemble the religious aspirations seen in a monastery.

Ōki comments, furthermore, on Hideo's image of van Gogh as follows:

> If we cannot call this a realist who did not allow the slightest abstraction, a seeker of the Absolute—then we may conclude that he felt with amazing integrity the Absolute forcibly penetrating his flesh and bones.

Ōki sees here not only Hideo's image of van Gogh but says Hideo's self-image, the other seeker of the Absolute, is superimposed on van Gogh's image. I feel that Ōki saw deeply into Hideo.

> Van Gogh's paintings, I feel, reflect a spirit far more than mere art works. I look beyond his paintings; I wait until I can feel the eyes behind the painting looking at me.

The reason is, I believe, that van Gogh's paintings represent a suffering soul prostrated before the Almighty.

After van Gogh began painting, he no longer believed in the church and the ministry. He ceased reading the Bible but did not necessarily dissociate himself from Christ. Ōki quotes from a letter van Gogh sent addressed to Emile Bernard.

> Christ alone—of all the philosophers, Magi, and so forth—has affirmed, as a principal certainty, eternal life, the infinity of time, the nothingness of death, the necessity and the *raison d'être* of serenity and devotion. He lived serenely, *as a greater artist than all other artists, despising marble and clay as well as color, working in living flesh.* That is to say, this matchless artist, hardly to be conceived of by the obtuse instrument of our modern, nervous, stupefied brains, made neither statues nor pictures nor books; he loudly proclaimed that he made—*living men*, living immortals.... These considerations, my dear comrade Bernard, lead us very far, very far afield; they raise us above

art itself. They make us see the art of creating life, the art of being immortal and alive at the same time.*

Ōki comments that Kobayashi perceived well the path that van Gogh said inevitably "leads us very far, very far afield" to "raise us above art itself". Next, Ōki quotes Hideo:

> The beauty of music infatuates man, which means he is astonished by the ear's capacity and marvels anew at man's spiritual powers. This leads us to rid ourselves of the illusionary, anxious and unstable self of the everyday—and to believe in another self that can listen to what is found in music.

Then Ōki comments, "The religious and the aesthetic unite, because both require abandoning the ego." Then he suggests that Kobayashi was the last person [in Japan] who attempted in the genre of criticism to unite aesthetics and religion.

I had considered Hideo's spirit of criticism in a religious, Christian sense, but Ōki understood it more deeply on the artistic and aesthetic levels; I believe Hideo would have found this more satisfying.

Furthermore, even my comments to Ōki on the words "The prideless will also fall" had been naïve. I simply said:

> We take comfort in interpreting in human terms the words "the prosperous will fall", "the rewards of cause and effect" and "virtue rewarded, and vice reproached". We think that by walking the righteous path, refraining from error, circumventing haughtiness and luxuries, we gain good fortune and happiness. TV dramas and novels, moreover, depict protagonists who find love and good will in the end, stirring the viewers and filling their hearts with contentment and hope—but are these actual? Are they not only deceptions? Those with pride or without pride are equally sinful, man is unable to judge what is right/wrong, good/bad or true/false in their unlimited complexities. Before God, the good and bad are equal, since the Biblical verse "Love thy enemy" holds true.

Ōki, however, saw more deeply, claiming as part of Hideo's faith at a deeper level the words "the prideless will also fall": "This statement refers to a historical truth; it is cruel and unreasonable—this is how Christians view history."

---

* Translation from *The Complete Letters*, Vol. III (London: Thames and Hudson, 1978), p. 498.

Here, Ōki agrees with Kobayashi that people had in the past misinterpreted the words "All is flowing and impermanent" because of their inability to bear and face it correctly, as Hideo had interpreted it. To bear this requires a Christ-like inner strength:

> The cross of Christ projects to the Jews and to all mankind the truth "the prideless also will fall". Then who are "the prideless"? Those like van Gogh who "willingly accepts his prescribed role as an insane person"; those who bear their own illnesses; the innocent children; and lastly Christ himself. Who are not "the prideless"? Those proclaiming themselves as "the prideless" or acclaiming their "saneness". Thinking themselves "the prideless", they become those "with pride", which is sin itself. To admit this sin means to accept a truth as penetrating as lightning—"the prideless will also fall"—and also not to avoid this fact. In the truth "the prideless will also fall", history touches eternity. That is the path the Absolute took.

Ōki summarizes his view as above and sees Christ's death and Resurrection in Hideo's beliefs, which I had never imagined.

Hideo discusses the anecdote "the prideless will also fall" of Dōkan, and then follows with other examples such as "Buddha's emptiness" and "Heraclitus' fire" in his essay "My View of Life".

> Buddha's discovery of the law of non-self probably never allowed him peace. He saw the fire mercilessly consuming people. He had probably concluded that only after allowing the fire to consume him could he deal with it, all other means having been indecisive. After all, hadn't the Phoenix flown up out of the ashes? Hadn't this fire without heart undeniably turned into a fire of compassion to eventually burn in the bosom of man? This defines Buddha's emptiness—which is my conclusion.

This undoubtedly was Buddha's emptiness, which some claimed ultimately became nihilism and atheism. But Ōki seriously considers Hideo's words—"Hadn't the Phoenix flown up from the ashes?"—as referring to God. If the Phoenix had been burnt in the fire of "the prideless also will fall" and if we believe that the Phoenix will fly up from the ashes, then it is the same as hoping for the miracle of Christ's death and his Resurrection. This movement of the spirit is surely close to Christianity, says Ōki.

I had been moved anew. Professor Ōki had read and probed deeply into Hideo's religion and faith; Hideo too had read into history, perceived into eternity and absorbed himself in religion deeply.

Hideo became fascinated with Rouault, who had inherited the craftsman spirit from his cabinet-maker father and been a stained-glass artisan since his youth. At around twenty, he entered art school and became a painter; but becoming a Christian in his middle years, he then concentrated in his later years on depicting Bible stories and Christ in the New Testament. Called a painter with a soul, much like van Gogh, Rouault deeply loved particularly the poor and the weak. In addition, applying his craftsman's diligence, passion and spirit of sacrifice, he pursued truth—attempting to depict a depth not readily visible to the human eyes. This trait, I think, Hideo admired in Rouault.

Once Hideo said to me: "I can well understand Rouault's faith, but not yours."

Ōki saw Hideo's image superimposed on van Gogh's, and in a similar way I see Hideo's image superimposed on Rouault's person and spirit. Aided by Chōzō Yoshii of the Yoshii Gallery, Hideo struggled to collect Rouault's paintings. I frequently saw one masterpiece, "Christ of Tiberia", painted by Rouault at around the age of seventy, when I visited Hideo's house. The old No. 12 size frame was impressive, but more so were the painting's beautiful evening sun reflecting on the sea, and the lonely white-robbed figure of Christ inside a rowboat. Fore and aft, Peter and Andrew crowded together as pure, strong figures. This was Rouault's foremost painting in Japan, Hideo used to say.

Another of Rouault's paintings depicted the Sea of Galilee, a woodblock print copy of a night scene with a darkish moon. Rouault's daughter, Izabelle, had signed it "To Hideo Kobayashi, in memory of my father."

When Hideo built his prefab house not too far from the entrance to the Hachiman Shrine, Izabelle Rouault presented him with an old, eighteenth-century colourful stained-glass piece. Each pane was beautifully stained, well positioned and interestingly shaped—all put together by Izabelle from panes her father had left over from his stained-glass making days. Izabelle's work was fixed to the window near the entrance, but she said on her visit there that the vertical and horizontal positions had been reversed.

Another painting that Rouault had taken ten years to complete Izabelle initially refused to sell, but Hideo insisted on purchasing it. The small painting shows only three faces on its crusted thick surface, oil-painted over and over. The central face of Christ is pale blue and grieving, and the other two men's faces appear on each side wearing large turbans. Wanting to identify the two, Hideo telephoned the author Shūsaku Endō. "Probably Caiaphas and Pilat," he replied.

After finishing his book *Motoori Norinaga* (1978), Hideo yearned to write on Rouault:

> Writing on Rouault means to write on Christ, but I can no longer afford at my age the time and energy required to go back to Christ. It's not possible. It's too late.

Then again, later, Hideo evidently said, "I understand now. Rouault had not depicted Christ—but painted in his scenes hypothetical images of Christ. Yes, that's it. With this understanding, I now feel I can write on Rouault."

Finally, however, his age did not allow him to.

Chapter 29
Thank You. Please Come Again

On 1 March 1983 at 1:40 am, Hideo's heart and breathing stopped. Having been told this day could perhaps be his last, the morning before I had packed my mourning dress and toiletries in a suitcase and headed for Keiō Hospital. There, Kiyomi, Haruko, her husband and Hideo's granddaughter were crowded in the room. Throughout that previous day we had watched Hideo's face as he slept soundly, his flushed face and peaceful sleep indicating he would live another day or two.

In the evening Haruko and the family said that they would leave for a while but would telephone me of any changes, so I too left for home. Late that night I was awakened by the phone. My husband, my son and I hurriedly sped by car to the hospital, but arrived too late.

His face in death looked handsome, but I felt a deep remorse, realizing that his firmly pressed mouth could no longer speak to me. Rather than finding myself shedding tears, I felt all my bodily strength suddenly leave me.

Placed at his pillow side was a cherry-blossom branch with two blossoms that were said to have bloomed unexpectedly just before Hideo took his last breath. It was Hideo's favorite *fugenzō* blossom that his friend Chōzō Yoshii had brought to the hospital ten days earlier, saying the still hard buds would blossom if placed next to Hideo. This we very much doubted, but just before he died the heated room perhaps had an effect and the buds unfurled their petals to the amazement of Kiyomi, Haruko and myself. Regrettably Hideo had missed seeing the blossoms, but I nonetheless sensed something of Hideo's lasting love for cherry blossoms there, leaving me with an inexplicable feeling.

For a long time, the loneliness, grief, chagrin, regret and disappointment all combined to sink heavily in my heart like lead.

The last time I had heard Hideo's usual clear and spirited voice had been on 23 December. Having been released from hospital, he was at his Kamakura home slowly recovering from his major operation in July.

At the end of September, just prior to his discharge, I had slowly walked him through the corridors of Keiō Hospital, holding his arm. As he stopped frequently to rest, I felt tears of joy well up in my eyes, seeing how much he wanted to recover.

After being discharged from hospital, he slowly regained his strength, until he was able to walk about the house and garden, but Kiyomi mentioned to me that his lack of appetite and small food intake might undermine his strength. Thinking that a nourishing meal for a change might give him strength, I remembered a friend who was fond of natural foods, especially unpolished rice.

Each time I visited her she had served me homemade meals, explaining their nutritious value and urging me to eat unpolished rice. The unpolished rice gruel with small beans in it had been especially delicious. She had once remarked how nourishing it was for a sick person with no appetite, so I quickly phoned her, asking her to prepare some for me to pick up on my way to Kamakura.

On 23 December she woke at 4 am and boiled for hours some unpolished rice gruel for me. I arrived with it just in time for Hideo's lunch. He had a spoonful at a time with the help of Kiyomi. He ate slowly, quietly and dutifully from the small bowl without commenting on how good or bad it tasted.

Hospitalized since the end of March, he had undergone daily examinations. Though only to check his stamina for a major operation, the physical strain had apparently been quite taxing. Emotionally, too, he was exhausted.

Quite despondently, he said, "They are checking the internal organs by taking photographs. Next, they'll probably start to take photos to check inside the brain."

As a result of the checkup, the operation took place in July and was a success. He recovered but was exhausted to the core, physically and emotionally. Whenever I visited him at the hospital, his face was flushed and he was always dozing. Occasionally he would wake up and acknowledge my presence with his expression. Then I always tried to speak to him but, at a loss for words, I only managed to utter, "You must be tired." He would nod and close his eyes again.

Earlier that morning before the rice-gruel lunch, for the first time since his release from hospital three months earlier, Hideo had gone out for a walk in the streets, with his son-in-law. This sign of health relieved me. After he returned from his walk, the barber came and groomed his hair to look neat at long last, but this had also fatigued him.

Just as at the hospital, I said, "You must be tired" while Hideo ate the unpolished rice gruel for lunch.

He answered in his clear, strong voice, as if irritated, "Yes, I am awfully tired."

Kiyomi said to me, pleased, that Hideo had surprisingly finished the whole bowl of unpolished rice gruel. I too felt this indicated the gradual return of his appetite, the intake of nourishment, and sufficient physical movement to regain his strength.

Finishing the rice gruel, he reclined in the Japanese-style room that commanded a direct view of the garden outside the sliding glass doors. Close by stood his favourite weeping plum tree and weeping cherry-blossom tree. On the plum tree branches, tangerine halves had been stuck here and there and two bulbuls flew to pick at them. Hideo took delight in watching the birds as he reclined in rest. A pair of bulbuls came every day, and picked at and consumed not only the tangerines but also the peelings. At times, sparrows came to chase off the bulbuls, perhaps to protect their territory.

Hideo loved the free small birds of nature. At his mountaintop house behind Hachiman Shrine, various birds had come to the garden lawn. I used to see starlings and bulbuls there, and Hideo had mounted a small birdhouse on the plum tree next to the veranda to enjoy watching tits flying there to lay eggs. Daily, he watched anxiously until the eggs hatched and the last tit had left the nest. Soon after, other tits would come to lay eggs; Hideo used to say, at times, they would be chased off by the sparrows.

Later that day, assured that he would see the plum and cherry blossoms next year, I went to the inner room before leaving. He had his eyes open wide, looking toward the garden.

I said, "I'll come again. Take care, and do try to recover."

He said "Oh, good, thank you, please come again," in his usual lively voice. Feeling encouraged, I left.

Soon after, Chōzō Yoshii had apparently brought over a painting by Cézanne titled "Forest", newly arrived from France at which Hideo quietly looked for a long time. In the days following, Hideo had apparently centred all his attention solely on this painting.

Then I was surprised to hear, in the New Year on 13 January, that Hideo had come down with a fever and had to be hospitalized. After that, his condition fluctuated; I visited him numerous times in the hospital. He would open his eyes wide and look at me with a nod; at other times, he merely responded with his eyes or remained asleep throughout. He was unable to speak or utter a sound. Then his soul came to rest in a faraway place.

Since his higher-school days, Hideo used to give me many scares. He escaped death due to a belated appendicitis operation; then he suffered from twisted intestines that worried me repeatedly; and after his marriage he incurred a serious ski injury; then he had to be hospitalized after falling off the platform of the war-torn Suidōbashi Station. He himself said, "I'm prone to injury."

I think it was only in his last ten years that I had been relieved from his frightening me with injuries and illnesses.

In these later years, he cared for his health and truly enjoyed his life. He often travelled with Kiyomi, going long distances to view cherry blossoms. He played golf almost until the day he was hospitalized—enjoying it like a child. He played also for health reasons.

After moving down from the mountaintop, he would wake early in the mornings to go for a walk on fine days, then have breakfast upon returning. He said that Kamakura still had many quiet roads suitable for walks. From Kamakura Station to Hideo's house, a narrow side street cobbled with old stones ran parallel to the main street; it was lined with cherry-blossom trees and led to Hachiman Shrine. I too used to enjoy taking this quiet side street. However, while Hideo was hospitalized, granite-concrete stones had replaced the old cobblestones.

Those days, Hideo filled his mornings with work, and again his afternoons—but he never worked in the evenings. He took an early evening bath, put on his *yukata* or kimono and enjoyed his evening sake. He would spend a long, leisurely suppertime. I went to Kamakura only once a month, but what was most enjoyable—and most instructive—was having evening sake with him, sitting directly opposite him. Hideo always insisted on tasty food, so only delicacies were arranged around his supper table.

Explaining each dish with relish, he would pour me sake from the pure silver kettle. Hideo loved this kettle, which had been offered as a golf prize by the writer Eiji Yoshikawa and won by Hideo.

Usually silent, as Hideo drank sake he began talking rapidly on many topics. Everything he said held something true and reverberated in me, as his teachings deeply penetrated me.

However, our evenings of sake drinking are now gone—and the opportunity to learn from him is no longer available.

Hideo's close friends all remark how Hideo had angrily shouted at and scolded them. I too was shouted at and scolded. However, this was out of his sincerity and affection, for which I must be thankful. I believe that everyone felt this way.

Hideo could not lie. Many considered him impudent, proud and disrespectful, but he was not. Rather, he was humble, I believe. That is, only a person who is genuinely humble is able to counter others with the truth. He was unable to flatter and sweet talk.

Hideo sought truth—believing in the truth, in the Absolute, and in miracles. So he probably rests alongside the Absolute now. However, he is no longer available to reprimand or scare me by doing the unexpected, and this indeed leaves me lonely and grieving.